Regie's Love

A Daughter of Former Slaves Recalls and Reflects

Regie Heard and Bonnie Langenhahn

McCORMICK & SCHILLING
Menomonee Falls, WI 53051

Regie's Love

A Daughter of Former Slaves Recalls and Reflects.

Copyright © 1987 by Regie Robinson Heard and Bonnie Langenhahn

FIRST EDITION

Published in the United States of America by McCormick & Schilling

cover art: Brandon Adams, Boehm & Associates, Inc.

LCC #87-061795

ISBN 0-9618212-1-3

Regie's Love is available for $8.95 ($7.95 plus $1.00 shipping) from:

McCORMICK & SCHILLING
Box 722
Menomonee Falls, WI 53051

Add sales tax where applicable.

Contents

PHOTOGRAPHS and DRAWINGS

FOREWORD

by Marilyn Bonjean, Ed. D.

Dr. Marilyn Bonjean is Director of Social Services at Marian Catholic Home, Milwaukee. She is a nationally recognized authority in the field of gerontology.

This book encourages us to look beyond a frail body and into the active mind behind the wrinkles — shattering the myth that age and institutional life suppress creativity, purpose and strength.

Regie's Love is an example of what writing therapy stimulation can create, and is a testament to the rich life experiences and wisdom that elderly persons can share with others. Unfortunately, this wealth often goes untapped because societal stereotypes teach us to undervalue contributions of older adults — especially nursing home residents.

Regie's co-author, Bonnie Langenhahn, uses writing therapeutically, building upon the older person's enjoyment of reminiscence. Such recollection helps aging people make sense of past successes and failures, resolve old conflicts, and deal with new ones.

The writer guides this process so that the person can focus on strengths and forgotten coping capabilities. Langenhahn's interviewing skills allow discussion of painful events, but focus on how this survivor coped. Reflection can help people to discover capable parts of themselves, and to apply forgotten strengths to current problems.

Nursing home residents are especially in need of a positive, solution-focused approach because physical frailty and the institutional regimen can diminish self-determination and self-esteem.

One resident described to me what she gained from the writing therapy program at Marian Catholic Home. "I tell her about my life — things that happened and my feelings. She puts it together into a story. I can pass that story on to my children and grandchildren because it is my legacy and their history. She asks questions that start me thinking. 'What did you learn from that experience?' or, 'How did you cope with those hard times?' Between our meetings, I remember all kinds of things I had forgotten. I'm learning more about me and what my life has meant. Sometimes I surprise myself with how much I've accomplished and how well I've managed through the years."

While Regie is a unique woman who has experienced a fascinating life, she is typical of many older adults who have so much to share.

As you read *Regie's Love,* think of those you know who could benefit from a writing therapy program. The program initiated at Marian Catholic Home by Bonnie Langenhahn could be replicated by staff and/or volunteers with writing skills.

- *If the resident doesn't know you, make a preliminary visit.* Tell the person that you help individuals to write journals about their lives. Reassure the person that the journal will be his or her personal property. You may expect to hear that some people feel their lives aren't important enough to warrant the effort. View this as an opportunity to reaffirm the worth of all individuals. When a person agrees to participate, establish a schedule of weekly meetings on the same day and time. Make a written appointment.

- *Arrive on time with a tape recorder.* It speeds the interview process and helps catch dialects and figures of decades-old speech. A recorder with a foot feed adapter will ease the subsequent job of transcribing.

- *Be natural and listen carefully.* You don't need a list of questions. Just begin with childhood memories, which are usually remembered as non-threatening and pleasant. Focus on one period of time, one incident, one personality sketch at a time. Share some incidents from your life to strengthen your relationship, but don't interrupt too much. Listen carefully. Learn to be comfortable with long pauses in conversation.

- *Rely on intuition and be flexible enough to make a leap in subject matter.* If you hear, "I can't think clearly today — I had the strangest dream last night," it isn't time to say, "That's too bad. What were you saying about your mother's garden?" If your friend wants to take you into a dream or spiritual experience, go! These dimensions are increasingly important to many adults.

- *Respect privacy; confidentiality is paramount in writing for others.* Don't pry, but do be receptive to the person's need to occasionally unburden past problems. If someone says, "Don't put this in," Don't! Turn off the recorder and seal the secret in your heart.

- *Pick up on positive statements.* When past loss or conflict results in tears, let your natural empathy take over. A non-judgmental, accepting attitude can be crucial to future communication. A simple touch may lead the person to forgiveness and self-acceptance.

- *Restrict interviews to one hour if the person is frail.*

- *When you transcribe your notes and tape, eliminate your motivating questions.* Include only the interviewee's words. What you don't write is as important as what you include. Written words take on a permanence that spoken words seldom do, so be acutely aware of the danger of hurting others. Family members will probably receive copies of the journal.

- *Most residents and their families are usually excited about the completed journals and wish to share them publicly.* In that case, be sure an impartial social worker receives the resident's written permission. Also, grant anonymity if desired.

ALSO ABOUT WRITING AS THERAPY:

THE WRITE AGE, First Magazine of Writing Therapy. By and for mature adults, physically impaired and gerontology professionals. Semiannual. ISSN 0892-9955 U.S. $9.50/year. McCormick & Schilling, Box 722, Menomonee Falls, WI 53051.

ACKNOWLEDGMENTS

Without suggestions and encouragement from family, friends and professionals, this work would have been less complete. Regie and I are indebted to my husband, Lyle, who proofread the book and lent support throughout the project, our daughters Anne, Ellen and Mary, my mother, Helene Grimstad, and Regie's son, Thomas Williams.

We also thank: Dr. Marilyn Bonjean, Director of Social Services, Merle McDonald, President, and Dorothy Tillman, aide of Marian Catholic Home; Mount Mary College departments of English and Behavioral Sciences, and Kathleen Buse, M.A., Director of Career Development; Joe and Anne Martinovich, for proofreading; Mary Medearis, Washington, Arkansas, Director of the Southwest Arkansas Regional Archives; Mildred Smith, Director of Washington's Black History Museum; and Mary Margaret Haynes, member of the first board of directors of the Foundation for the Restoration of Pioneer Washington. — B.L.

EDITOR'S NOTE ABOUT PSEUDONYMS

Where necessary, place names have been regretfully omitted (i.e., the plantation where the slave, Becky, Regie's great-grandmother, gave birth to Dr.W's sons). Old Arkansas news articles and the first census records to include former slaves after the Civil War (from Hempstead County Archives in Washington), corroborate places and names that Regie's mother passed to her. Becky was probably in her teens when Dr.W. migrated to southwestern Arkansas about 1830 and began acquiring slaves and growing cotton. She may have given birth to Edmund during that time: he was listed as a thirty-eight-year-old "mulatto" in the 1870 census. Records were often inaccurate, but Edmund and James were probably born before 1845, when Dr.W. married the widow who owned the plantation where Becky was a slave (named by Regie, affirmed by archives).

Because Regie wanted to contribute to minority history of the post-Reconstruction South, as many names as possible were retained. Where delicate subject matter dictated, pseudonyms were given and are indicated by asterisks (*). Similarity to names of real persons, living or dead, is coincidental.

for
Mama,
Grandma,
Mary Ann
and all invisible women
who scatter seeds of
Love-consciousness
on Planet Earth

Entrance to the plantation where Regie's mother, grandmother Susan and great-grandmother Becky were slaves.

1

Family:
Slaves, Indian, Irishman

"My arm was danglin' and I was screamin' with the pain and cryin' for mama. Then the doctor put a soaked rag smelled funny over my face. Last I 'member, mama was standin' behind the doctor, wipin' her eyes in her apron."

Mama quit talking and looked up from her mending. She gazed off like I wasn't sitting on the floor beside her. Nice days, she was on her feet from sunup to sundown. Washing, cooking, cleaning, picking. Mama's life. Wet days like this, she sat.

Outside, a drizzle made the leaves of the trees rustle quiet as palmetto fans in church. Even if I hadn't heard the leaves, I'd have known it was raining. I could smell the worms. Rain made the worms come up and the snakes go down. And it made mama sit and mend or piece quilts. And tell stories.

Mama's hands were nearly white against the faded blue shirt she was mending. She and papa had a good portion of white blood in them and we were as light as the sand above the gullies at the edge of Washington in southwestern Arkansas.

"What happened then, Mama?" I said, knowing full well what happened then. I'd heard the stories of mama's and papa's childhoods during Reconstruction after the Civil War.

"Regina, you sure are fulla big questions for a small child!" she laughed. "Guess I can tell you one more time...

"I knew something was dreadful wrong. My mama, your Grandma Susan, never shed a tear unless somebody died. But even if she hadn't a been crying, I'd a known somethin' was wrong cuz I'd watched 'em washin' and scorchin' that knife in the fire and I could see it on the table. I seen mama crying and that knife a gleaming afore the doctor held me down and

3

slapped that rag over my face.

"'Breathe deep, 'Melia, breathe in deep, chil' an' ya'll take a nice nap. Won't know what touched ya,' he said.

"His cheeks was wet from tears and his eyes was sad as Job's. Then I went to sleep. Seemed like I had a nightmare then and I heard someone screamin' and screamin' and my arm was hotter'n scaldin' water."

I dabbed at my eyes and mama leaned over, pulled another shirt from the basket, then hunched over it, clamped the torn cuff against her leg with the stump of her right arm and pulled the cuff taut with the side of her left fist.

"When I woke up, your gramma was sitting there with a cup of soup," mama continued. "She leaned down to feed me and after a few sips I tried to reach up to help myself." Mama's voice grew quiet as the rain outside. "That's the first I knew my arm was gone. All's was there was this stump wrapped in bloody rags." Mama raised her half-arm. "I started sobbin' so's I lak ta choked. My mama told me ta 'Hush, chil', hush!' real tender. She put down the soup and held me, but I could feel her a shakin'. We sat there shakin' and moanin' and holdin' each other tight till we got wore out and went to sleep. Ever after, seemed like I could feel my fingers reachin' right out for that soup..."

"What'd they do with it, Mama?" I said. "What'd they do with the arm?"

"Lan' sake, Regina, you do ask questions! Seems ta me I've told you a hundred times!" mama smiled, but didn't take her eyes off her mending. "All's I know is, your gramma said they buried it somewhere so's I wouldn't get the burning pains. 'Them that's had their cut-off limbs burned has the burnin' pains resta their lives,' your gramma said. 'Gets 'em where the arm or leg used to be. Happen to a pack a slaves, happen to a pack a soldiers in the war,' she said. I imagine she meant Confederates. Those was the ones we most knew about but she mighta known some Yankees up on Justus Hill—that was named after John Justus used to own the mill. Your gramma never showed me where my arm was buried and I didn't trouble her about it. Maybe the vultures got it. Lord knows, there's enough of 'em around! Truth be, I didn't want to know."

The leaves on the trees had stopped rustling and mama put the mending in the basket.

"Regina, the rain's stopped," she said, jumping up from the chair. "Go get the water for that hambone!"

Reluctantly, I trudged outside and slipped and slopped toward our well. Sandy slime oozed between my toes like healing balm and I wiggled my feet to see how many kinds of tracks I could make...

On other rainy days mama told about our ancestors. My brothers and sisters weren't interested in family stories, but I waited for the sky to turn cloudy!

In 1859 mama was born a slave, Amelia W___, to Edmund and Susan W___ on a prosperous plantation in Hempstead County, Arkansas. But she didn't feel like a slave because she lived in the big house and was pampered because she was crippled. Grandma Susan was a house slave there; she was never a fieldhand because she was part French-Indian and very light, but she had some African blood or she wouldn't have been a slave. "Mulatto," they called her. She worked in the big house and did fine sewing for Mrs. W___ and she, Grandpa Edmund and their family stayed on after the war. There were four children: Ernest, Jason, Amelia (mama) and Minnie.

Mama was about eight when she fell from a tree and lost her arm. The doctor thought she'd sprained it but it got worse and then he said it was broken. By then poisoning had set in, so mama was crippled and her owners pampered her.

"Oh, they was good to me," mama said. "Treated me like one of them. Your gramma, too. I can remember Mrs. W___ and my mama talking and joking like friends when no company was around."

Someone in the big house taught mama to read and she read anything she could lay her hand on until the day she died, but she never learned to write because she wanted to write with the hand she'd lost. To me, she was the strongest woman in the world, and I loved her so much that when she'd get a headache, I'd get one, too!

My great-grandmother on Grandpa Edmund's side (mama's father) was a slave named Becky who worked on the plantation. At some point in the 1830's or 1840's, a white man named Dr. W___ came to the plantation and proceeded to take a slave woman for his mistress: my great-grandmother Becky. She had two sons by Dr. W___—Edmund and

5

James—and Edmund, the firstborn, was mama's father and my grandfather.

Whether Becky came before or after his marriage, I don't know, but long before mama was born Dr. W___ had married the wealthy widow who owned the plantation. Cotton was king then in Hempstead County and he became a rich man.

Dr. W___ recognized his sons by Becky, and took Edmund and James with him when he went out with the horse and buggy. When he got old he was kind of crazy and so fat, most of the time he wore what they called a "Mother Hubbard," and he wanted James with him all the time.

"James! James!" he'd call. I remember Great Uncle Jim's family very well because we used to visit his daughter (mama's cousin), Mary, at her home in Ozan.

A few years after the Civil War ended, one of Mrs. W___'s sisters took mama to Washington to work for her, and that's where mama met papa.

PAPA

My father's name was Noble Robinson, but everyone called him "Nobie." Papa was part Indian and quiet around us kids, but mama told me he was born in slavery in Montgomery, Alabama. Papa's mother had been taken from Baltimore to Alabama and I don't know how she came to Arkansas—maybe she was sold. Delphia Gaines was a slave even though she was supposed to be all Cherokee Indian, and she was stern and unaffectionate. Papa had two brothers, Wiley and Benjamin.

Papa was silent and serious like his mother. He was tall, handsome and looked Indian but we were almost afraid of him because he was so stern.

Papa was in slavery until he was eleven, living in his master's big house on a Washington plantation and caring for his master's child. After the war ended, the federal government sent Union troops to the South to keep order because southerners had given up their citizenship and white Nightriders were terrorizing and killing former slaves. Papa was tending this white child when the Union troops come to Washington. They were blowing their horns in all their pretty uniforms and they bib-walked up to Justus Hill, out past the old courthouse that had been turned into the Confederate

6

state capitol.

The day the Yankees came, papa set that child down on the street and followed the soldiers up to their camp. He hung around the soldiers on Justus Hill, fetching water and running errands to earn some good currency. The soldiers came because the South was in turmoil.

"There was more burnin', lootin' and killin' than you'd ever want to know about, Regina," mama said. "But things was pretty peaceful around Washington. Folks here always been peace-lovin'."

Because he was the youngest son, Ben Gaines was able to go to school, but papa had to work to help his mother, and at night Ben taught him his ABC's. Papa was working, listening and learning things from the Yankee soldiers and an officer by the name of Captain Robinson took a liking to him. He was kind to papa and helped him with his reading; my father looked up to the Captain so, he took his name. That's where our name of Robinson came from. After my father learned to read he studied on his own, even studied some law later. He read all of his life and had a large collection of fine old books at home.

After the war, life was hard for blacks and whites. The plantations and stores began to slide downhill without slaves and money. I think it was then that a lot of white folks moved to Hope and pretty soon Hope was bigger than Washington. The northern white people tried to educate the Negroes because they were turned loose and had no place to go. Many stayed on working like they had because they had nothing else to do. As the plantations broke down, a lot of them began to sharecrop: Hempstead County was big cotton country.

Papa learned enough to teach in little country schools for the Negro children. And he worked in politics. He was a constable before I was born and a deputy sheriff for years. He had an old paper showing that he was constable, and an old poll tax paper. One year he was a representative to the Arkansas Republican Convention; he was a leader for colored people in the county. Anytime they had paperwork, they came to papa. He wrote beautifully and signed his name "N. B. Robinson." He joked that his name was Napolean Bonaparte!

Any kind of trouble, they all came to him. Many times when country boys were in jail, papa mortgaged our house for bail. And he was a deputy sheriff until he got too old to ride a horse, after I was a grown woman. Either I wasn't born or I was too little to remember the year when a dreadful thing happened while he was a deputy.

"One day your papa come gallopin' into the yard late and walked into the kitchen lookin' like the world was on his shoulders," mama told me. "'Whatever's the matter, Nobie?' I asked him.

"'They're saying one of my old pupils murdered a white child down near Paris and there's a warrant out,' your papa said. With the state line so close, he thought the boy might be heading toward Washington, and there was a big reward out. 'Blood'll be shed over this one!' your papa said. 'Just hope he doesn't head this way!'"

A day or two later my father was out riding, looking for a man who'd jumped a gambling debt. Papa was going through the woods when suddenly the boy came out from the trees.

"Please help me, Mr. Robinson!" he said. "Take me in! I did somethin' awful an' I'm tired a runnin'."

He was weak, dirty, scratched up and scared. My father didn't want the boy to surrender to him because he knew what they'd do to him, but papa took him to the jail. Papa sent a wire to Paris, Texas, and the authorities there requested him and the U. S. Marshall to take the youth to Paris. They promised that they wouldn't do anything to the boy, said they'd let the law take its course.

So papa left for Texas with the boy shackled to him and to U. S. Marshall Henry Holman. (One of my brothers was named after him, he and papa were so close.) After they got to Paris, the authorities manhandled them something awful. Then they took the boy and burned him at the stake, right where they stood. My father never got over it. His hair turned white afterwards and he wouldn't take the reward.

At home, the silent Indian part of papa came out, but when he was younger he'd make a speech at the drop of a hat at public meetings. Being part Indian and well-read, papa didn't fit in with white or black society, but the poor people around Washington thought he was a god.

8

2

Seasons of Childhood —

1898-1907:
Washington, Arkansas

Washington was all green rolling hills, red clay gullies and sugar-white sand. It had the biggest magnolia tree in the United States, like an oak the trunk was so big. People said the seed had been planted by Grandison Royston, the father of old Captain Royston up the street. In summer we could smell the magnolias for miles.

Besides the Royston carriage house, the courthouse was the only brick building in town. It was about four blocks from our place and sat on a square enclosed by a white wooden fence with two stiles in front. Washington was the county seat of Hempstead County and court was held in spring and fall, one for civil and one for criminal cases. Criminals were held at the jail two or three blocks from the courthouse, then hung on courthouse square.

One day my youngest brother raced in, put on clean overalls and ran out the door with mama calling after him.

"Ben! Where d'you think you're going?" she called.

"To the hanging," he yelled, "for a piece of rope!"

"Oh, dear Lord!" mama whispered, then glanced at my sister Minnie and me. "I'm prayin' for the souls of them's goin' to depart," she said.

I didn't know what a "soul" was, but I was sure that Depart must be a bad place because mama looked sad. Only I couldn't figure out why so many people were laughing and going in the same direction as Ben. About an hour later he ran in twirling a piece of rope.

"Three at once!" he said. "Hung three at once!" He lifted his eyebrows and tried to look big but his eyes looked scared.

9

"Get in the other room, young man!" mama said. She grabbed our shoulders and turned Minnie and me toward the door. "And you go out and play!"

Any time things got interesting in the house, mama sent us outside. And when grown-ups were talking outside on the walk or porch, she sent us inside.

Later, I found out that after someone was hung, the rope was cut into little pieces for souvenirs for the spectators. The day Ben went, there was a big crowd. But with three ropes, there were enough pieces to go around.

GAINING A DREAM, and LOSING A BROTHER; THE GALVESTON FLOOD

Papa and mama were married in 1874, the same year the brick courthouse was built; he was twenty and she was fifteen. They had eleven children but they only raised nine. Susan, the third child, got a grain of corn stuck in her windpipe and the doctor slit her throat, but she choked to death. Another infant died, then I was born September 20, 1894, second to the youngest. We were two-and-a-half to three years apart—I reckon the Lord spaced us that way for our mother. My oldest sister Mozelle was already married when I was born; Ben was the only brother at home and he left when he was eighteen.

Mama had lots of magazines and I looked at the pictures of teashops with china, linens and silver and thought how wonderful it would be to own such a place. That was my dream. Wasn't papa's sister the head cook in a hotel in Hope? A dream of a teashop might not come true but it wouldn't hurt anyone if I kept dreaming. I'd never heard of a place called "Milwaukee."

Most afternoons I had my nose in a book after I learned to read and at night we played hide-and-go-seek outside by the light of the moon until mama called. We went barefoot and hated to go in because we had to wash our feet before we went to bed.

Our mother gave us a lot of freedom and every child she had was crazy about her. We'd be playing while she did dishes alone. But if we were mischievous and pushed her real hard I thought she'd try to kill us when she whipped us. "Shit the devil!" she said when she was mad and used a switch from a peach tree or whatever was handy. Most of the time she was good-natured and I never saw her having any over-the-fencerail fussing at the neighbors. Everybody loved her.

As for the boys, papa disciplined them. One thing that was sad for my father, the boys never wanted an education and they never got beyond eighth grade when they lit out, ran to Kansas City and all.

My brother Allen was mischievous and always getting into trouble. One time papa had trimmed some trees and Allen made a slide out of the brush like an Indian travois. I was a little tyke and he sat me on top of a bush he'd tied to our mustang, Bill. Bill was wild and he ran away with me bouncing behind on the bush until I fell off. "Got such a cut under your eye it's a wonder it didn't put your eye out!" mama told me when I was bigger.

Papa gave Allen a licking for that. Another time he got in trouble papa whipped him and Allen ran away for good. Papa grieved about that all of his life. In 1900 we had a letter from Allen saying he was going to Galveston, Texas. That was just before the flood when an old colored lady was walking the streets of Galveston for days, preaching and prophecying.

"You better leave! You better leave!" she warned. "This town is going to be destroyed!" Everybody laughed and called her "crazy," and you can find it in history that a giant tidal wave came out of the bay and flooded Galveston. Thousands of people were destroyed.

We never heard from Allen after that. He only wrote that one letter. Forty years later after papa was old and came to Milwaukee, he'd still sit and read that letter, it grieved him so.

The economy had changed with the end of slavery and people couldn't keep up the plantations, so in my childhood parts of Washington were run-down. Houses that burned weren't re-built and there were vine-covered mansions in ruins all around. The two-story Royston house up the street was the finest place

11

left, with a veranda and big columns across the front. In 1880 the population had been at its peak—780—but many former residents moved and formed a new town about eight miles away called Hope.

Our townspeople were friendly and everybody knew everybody. The Colored Methodist Episcopal church was across the road from our house and next to it was a white Presbyterian parsonage. The Presbyterian minister got the WASHINGTON TELEGRAPH (Will Etter's newspaper) and saved them and gave them to papa to read. Up the hill lived Mr. Stewart Monroe, the county clerk. There was no segregated housing. We just didn't visit white people.

"Y'all go to the back door when you deliver berries," mama said. Going to white people's houses always meant going to the back door.

There were a lot of former slaves and each January 1 they had an Emancipation Proclamation Day parade. Sometimes we had nice weather and the band marched around town in front of the wagons and buggies. The white people enjoyed it and stood on the corners to watch.

Everything I learned about slavery was through my mother and old people. I liked to talk to old people and old people like Rob Samuels liked to talk to me. He'd been county clerk and was the son of Richard Samuels, one of our first black politicians during Reconstruction. He'd served in the state legislature and was Miami Davis' stepfather. Miami and her husband ran the hotel, The Davis House.

Before papa bought our house, we rented the old Samuels' house at the edge of town where Richard Samuels was buried. Rob Samuels and his wife, Sarah, were our nearest neighbors. She was part Indian, like we were, and I never saw her leave the house. Their daughter Lela was always saying she saw the ghost of her grandpa walking around after he died. The official story was that Richard Samuels' body wasn't brought into town for a funeral because he died of smallpox, but some people said he died a mysterious death and that the house was haunted.

Rob Samuels was a tall old man with a white beard. Sometimes when I'd be coming up the road, he'd be going down and he'd stop to talk and I thought it was wonderful that he'd talk to me, a child, even though it was mostly about politics. Sometimes he'd mention "lily white

12

Republicans" and I'd wonder what he meant—papa said Negroes were Republicans.

Of course, I learned the most about slavery from mama. She taught me a lot of things. In spring she took us to pick dewberries on vines in the gullies. The dogwood bloomed early and the trees were filled with white blossoms. There were jonquils, violets and hyacinths, miles and miles of them. The air was fine-smelling with flowers, and old vacant houses were covered with blossoms blotting broken windows and peeling paint. Sometimes we could see former slaves moving around in a room of a deserted mansion they'd occupied.

After dewberries came blackberries, then blueberries. There'd be a thicket of woods here and hollows there, but when we went to pick berries we'd go to the "bottom" creek-land where farmers planted crops. Mama canned and we sold five-gallon buckets of blackberries for a quarter at white folks' back doors.

A favorite time was visiting grandma. Grandpa Edmund had died and Grandma Susan's name was "Dixon" by the time I was born. Columbus was about ten miles away but it seemed like a hundred miles because we went by horse and buggy. About once a month, early on the morning we were leaving for grandma's, papa went to the livery stable. It was owned by a German immigrant named Von Jagerfield, a distinguished man who carried a small whip and wore a riding habit with a black velvet jacket and black-billed cap. Papa'd rent a horse and buggy and come home for us. Papa and mama climbed up in front on the seat and Bessie, Minnie and I plopped down behind them on a box or stool on the floor of the buggy. One time when papa hit the horse and yelled, "Giddyap!" the horse reared and Bessie fell out. We all laughed, even Bessie.

Then we bumped over the rutted road past woods, cotton fields and old mansions that had been grand plantations, until we came to grandma's little house at the edge of Columbus. When we got near her place we could see a table brimming with food in her front yard; although she was old and not well she'd have a big feed in front of her house. I thought grandma was the prettiest, greatest person on earth. All her neighbors loved her, too, including white teen-agers. At grandma's our aunts and uncles fussed over us. Or over Bessie.

"I do declare, Bessie, you're prettier every day!"

"Takes after Amelia and gramma."

"Regina, you still head of your class? Got a mind like your papa!"

Wasn't much breath wasted on my looks. My sister-in-law always said, "Bessie's so pretty and Reg is so ugly!" That followed me all my life. I didn't resent Bessie's being pretty, didn't even resent her saying that, but it made me feel like an underdog and I think that's why I was afraid of things. If I had to go up town alone and saw people down the street, I'd go around the block to keep from having to pass them.

We'd moved around a lot when papa was teaching in different towns and before he bought our house we lived in a place that had glass panels on each side of our front door. I was a little girl when I'd stand looking at my image in that glass, wondering who I was or what I was, and I sensed there must be something more important in life than what we saw around us.

But mama's sister, Aunt Minnie, made me feel special. They lived on a farm in the hills and their boys were grown so they had one of us each summer. At Aunt Minnie's I was the only child, and did I live it up! In the hills near the farm were artesian wells where people did their laundry. One day everybody'd go up in wagons, build fires under old black pots with feet and visit while they boiled clothes.

At home, where papa cut wood there'd be a lot of chips that mama swept and burned under our wash pot. Sometimes she set the chips on fire in the yard and said, "Smoke will follow the one that's prettiest!" She'd be sweeping the yard, burning chips, and we'd be running through the smoke!

When my brothers were home they caught rabbits, possums and coons. If one of them caught a possum he put it in a box for awhile, claimed it was to clean it out because possum ate carrion. Once Ben had a possum in a box and I was playing, poking a stick at it.

"Betcha don't know where I found him!" Ben teased.

"Don't know's I care!" I said.

"Caught him settin' on a old dead horse!" Ben doubled up with laughter. After that I never ate possum again.

We had good eating, though. Papa gardened and raised chickens, hogs and a few beef cattle. Daisy, our Jersey cow, had a calf called Princess that was a great big thing I'd carry around with my arms under her front legs, her hind legs dragging on the ground. The cows could wander all over town because Daisy knew when to come and where she lived. If anyone had a dry cow the neighbors helped out and gave that family buttermilk.

We'd had good luck with chickens so one year papa decided to raise turkeys; he bought turkey eggs and we put them under big hens to hatch. Five or six turkeys hatched and walked around and then we'd see one with its head drooping. The next thing, it'd be dead on the ground. We didn't raise one—they all died.

A white lady in the country had fine ducks and sold duck eggs for a big price, two dollars a dozen, so we bought a dozen and not one of them hatched. We thought she did something to them because when we stuck a pin in them we could tell they weren't fertile.

FOURTH OF JULY BARBECUE

In early summer, there was always a big race to see who could raise the biggest watermelon by the Fourth of July. One year, papa had a champion Tom Watson melon that was close to one hundred pounds.

On the Fourth we had free barbecue on the edge of town, at the foot of Justus Hill. Farmers and store owners gave beef, hogs and sheep to be skewered on poles and laid over long, deep trenches in the ground. Mama's cousin, Uncle Richard Johnson, did most of the barbecuing, and the meat'd be cooking all night while we were smelling all night!

By the light of the pit fires, Bessie, Minnie and I'd go down, watch and walk around sniffing. We'd watch and smell awhile, then run around and play hide 'n seek with our cousins. Near noon on the Fourth, the men and women piled meat, pickles, beans, fresh baked bread and watermelons on long boards laid across wooden horses. That was real barbecue!

Negroes and Whites were served separately and they ate separately. They never mixed, but they never fought. There were two sets of tables: one at one end of the grounds for Whites, one at the other end for Negroes. At that time, we didn't think anything of it because we all had fun.

15

FALL: JUMPING ON MELONS, PET ON A PLATTER

In fall we picked hickory nuts and scaly barks with mama. Scaly barks grew on trees with rough bark and were kind of like hickory nuts, but they had thin shells and we could crack them with our teeth—I reckon that's why I've got false teeth now! We picked chinquepins, too, that looked like hazelnuts and had stickers.

Watermelons were left in the fields and after the first frost when we were picking nuts we'd go through the fields, jump on the melons and bust them open with our feet. Then we'd eat out the hearts, cold as ice.

In our back yard we made an arbor out of poles and branches to put collard greens under to keep for winter. We had peas called "White Lady Peas" that we joked about: "Did you ever see a White Lady Pea on the table?"

Every year papa bought shoats to slaughter in fall and, knowing they were going to be killed, Bessie and I'd get the little pigs for pets. After they were grown papa hired someone to go way back in the yard to kill them—he never did it. My last pet pig got so big they couldn't kill him by hitting his head with an ax so they had to shoot him. The guy that did it wasn't a good shot and just wounded him. My pig ran around squealing so loud, I tore into the house and hid my head.

"I won't eat him! I'm not gonna eat him!" I cried. A few days later mama was frying him out and the air hung sweet with smells of pork. That night I trudged to the table with my head down, but when they passed the platter of that fine smelling meat I ate as many chops as anybody else. But I never had another pet pig.

CHRISTMAS: ARTHUR DUCKETT AND A SLOPJAR

A few days before Christmas mama and the older children and I would put on our coats and walk to the woods near our house to hunt for a holly tree, smilax and mistletoe. Smilax was a glossy-leaved vine that grew in trees and we skipped along looking for vines. "There's smilax!" somebody would yell and point. We'd run and watch one of the older children climb a tree and yank the vine from the limbs. When it fell we all scrambled and soon our arms were loaded with green garlands.

Mistletoe was more scarce and harder to find because it grew in the tips of the trees. While we were hunting for smilax and mistletoe we kept our eyes on the holly trees so we'd know where the biggest ones with the most berries were. We'd spot one and when we came back Ben would begin swinging the ax and soon we'd marching home with our tree and smilax.

Back home, mama and my older sisters fastened the vines near the top of the ceiling so that they hung down covering the walls, making the living room a living green, with the berry covered tree in the corner. We said we couldn't get enough in a stocking, so on Christmas Eve we put big shoeboxes by the fireplace for "Sandy Claws" to fill. In the morning we ran in to find fruit, nuts, candycanes and a doll. When we were lucky we got a pair of high-buckled shoes, but one year times were lean and papa only brought home a sack of apples.

On Christmas children would sneak up to a neighbor's house and yell, "Christmas gift!" Samuels always pretended that they hadn't seen us before we yelled, so they'd have to give us candy or fruit.

We went to the Methodist church on Christmas night, when young people put presents under the tree. Then someone called the names tied onto them. We girls were always hoping to get something from under the tree, knowing we weren't going to because we hadn't put anything there!

I was in my early teens the year Arthur Duckett from Ashdown was courting Daisy Carter. I was sitting with my girl friends and the church was full when the boys were taking presents up.

"Here come Arthur Duckett!" someone whispered.

"Can ya see what he's carryin'?" I said.

"Lord, if it's what I think it is, Daisy lak ta die!"

"Look lak a china slopjar ta me!"

"—with flowers on it!"

The year that Arthur Duckett strolled up and stuck a flowered slopjar and chamber under the Christmas tree for Daisy Carter became history around Washington. Everybody talked and laughed about it for years, but Daisy forgave him: they got married.

Outside after church the men shot Roman candles and fireworks. We didn't have fireworks on the Fourth of July, but we had them for Christmas. Especially the year that Arthur Duckett came from Ashdown.

3

"Hanted" House, To Lighting Up the Town

Some coachwhip snakes had a nest in the roots of an old tree at the front gate of our house and they'd crawl all over the yard. "Better look out, dey whip yo' ta death, dey catch ya!" Aunt Mary B. said. She wasn't our aunt but everybody was "aunt" or "uncle." Aunt Mary was a rough old lady who knew what she was talking about and we listened to what she said.

Someone said the house we bought was on Izzard Street but we never used street names. In summer, from our porch we could hear preaching and dozens of versions of the same hymn at the Methodist church across the street. Our house had an open hall and four rooms, enough space for mama, papa and four of us—Jennie, Minnie, Bessie and me.

Under the clapboards of our home was a log cabin that had sat at the crossroads of the old Southwest Trail and the Military Road where thousands of Choctaws and Chickasaws had been forced to march west in the 1830's, beyond Arkansas Territory. President Andrew Jackson had ordered that all Indians east of the Mississippi be moved west, and a lot of Washington plantation owners got rich by setting up stands and selling their corn and cattle to the government agents in charge of the caravans of cold, sick, dying Indians—they hauled those dying of cholera in wagons.

Many people lived in the cabin over the years and old-timers said a fat lady died in it, got out of bed and died on the floor. She was so big, people on the street could hear her breathing when she died.

Everybody said our house was "hanted," maybe by her. One sunny morning Aunt Mary B. was on the porch with mama.

Nobody was in the house, but mama heard heavy breathing, like light snoring, coming from inside.

"What dat noise? Who be sleepin' dis time a day?" Aunt Mary asked.

"Nobody," mama said. "I don't hear anything." But she could hear the breathing.

There were other incidents. One Friday night Jennie, Minnie and some girl friends were waiting for boys to call to take them to a school social. Papa, mama, Bessie and I were in the other room when the girls screamed and we heard banging. We ran in and they were shaking and screaming. The windows were down low but something from outside had reached through the glass and pulled the shade down. When the girls tried to run out, the door slammed in against them. Someone ran and got Mozelle's husband from the Methodist parsonage next door, and he and papa went all around the house and yard but they didn't see anyone.

Joe and Emma Green were friends of mama's who lived outside of town and sometimes she'd visit them. Emma was crippled but they were well off because Joe had a kiln for making bricks, mainly for wells. When mama was late coming home we'd be in front of our house waiting for her because we were afraid to go inside!

I never went to public school but one day in my life. I didn't know we couldn't talk out loud so I was talking, and the next I knew Miss Curry was standing over me with a switch! She made me go to a corner and scared me half to death. When school was out Jennie lit out running home to tell papa and mama.

"Shoulda seen Miz Curry holdin' the switch over her!" Jennie said.

"I don't wanna go to school!" I wailed.

"Sounds like Miz Curry don't have good understandin'," mama said.

"Maybe Miz Curry'll get understandin' when the Robinson girls don't come back," papa said. "Anyhow, Haygood's a better school."

"HAYGOOD!" Jennie shrieked.

"You mean I don't hafta go back?" I said.

20

"Public school's loss is Haygood's gain!" Papa smiled.

The next day he enrolled us at Haygood Seminary on the other side of town, on the road to Fulton—that was where they made moonshine like "Red Eye" and "White Mule" on an island in the Red River. Established for black students by the Colored Methodist Episcopal Church, Haygood went from the grades through high school. Professor George Tyus was president and I'd never do anything wrong so he'd have to scold, I respected him so.

When we'd come home from school mama always had a pot on the stove. We tossed our books aside and ran to see what she'd fixed. Peas? Spareribs? Turnip greens? We didn't even take time to take off our hats before we ate!

Nothing could daunt our mother. When we ran out of lamp oil she took us into the woods for pine nuts. At home we lit them in the fireplace and the burning resin made a sweet pine smell and a strong light to read by. While we were doing homework we put sweet potatoes in the hot ashes and ate them when we finished our lessons.

"Know when the potatoes's done?" Jennie asked.

"When?" I said.

"Gotta watch the steam, the stuff looks like mist on a still mornin'," Jennie said. "Gotta watch for when it comes out in short busts. When the steam comes in busts, potatoes's done." So when we heard the sweet potatoes sizzling we looked up from our books and watched for the first bursts of steam. Then we ate!

We were poor but we always ate well and never thought of ourselves as poor. We had love, a clean home, time to play and time at night to listen to the boys in the band that papa directed practicing next door in the old Methodist parsonage. Twins Louis and Eugene Tyus and Moten Thomas were my friends, but we giggled and plugged our ears, the band was so bad. Papa played coronet and directed and the boys were afraid of him, he was so strict.

FORMER SLAVES IN AN OLD MANSION

We also had time to listen to former slaves tell stories. The old Bolden sisters had moved out of a mansion at the edge of town when they couldn't care for it anymore. It had been a

21

fine estate but it was deserted until an ancient slave called Uncle Marshall and his son, Sam, moved in downstairs. My sister Mozelle and her preacher husband, C. S., lived upstairs there when they were first married and that's how I met Uncle Marshall and Sam.

One summer Minnie, Bessie and I had to take turns staying with sister because C. S. was gone a lot and mama sent us out to stay with Mozelle. The Bolden gravelot was in the backyard, fenced in and a tangle of weeds and wildflowers, and we ran between headstones, scared each other and looked at markers. I know I was nearly twelve because my period began at Mozelle's. It happened at night.

I woke up and thought something terrible was happening. I didn't know what to do because mama had never told me anything, so I curled up and prayed I wouldn't die, talked to the Lord most of the night. In the morning I washed quickly and dressed. Maybe if I acted normal I wouldn't die. Mozelle was making beds and called me into the bedroom.

"Regina, honey, you ever menstruate before?" she said.

"What's that?" I asked.

Sister smiled and we sat down on the edge of the bed.

"Looks like we've got some talkin to do..." she said.

That's how I remember how old I was the summer I stayed in the old Bolden place.

Little Uncle Marshall was about a hundred years old, blind and felt his way around with a stick. Sam was chunky-set, balding and jolly, always telling jokes. He loved to tell a story of how during slavery some masters allowed their slaves to steal food from other slaveowners.

"Dey mastuhs didn' mind 'em killin' someun's cow or hog if dey could get by with it, even let 'em hang 'em in dey own smokehouse," Sam chuckled. "One night it be dark as a cave and the cows is layin' down when dese slaves gonna steal a calf. Dey sneaks up 'n hits the calf ober da head with a hatchet and it jumps up whinnyin' cuz da calf dey hits is a white man's racehoss colt! Thieves run outa dat pasture fast as any racehoss!" Sam told lots of stories.

He had to do everything for Uncle Marshall, even cook in a cast iron kettle he put in coals. The fireplace was so huge he could put full logs in and there'd still be room. Sam would put a lid on the pot, put hot coals on top of that and bake anything, even cakes. For ash cake he made stiff cornmeal batter, rolled it up and put it in hot ashes to bake. It made a crust on the outside and when it was done the old men ate everything but the crust, like they were scooping out the insides of a sweet potato.

REVIVALS

It was an old-time thing when a preacher got to shouting and carrying on at a revival.
"Are you sinners?"
"Yeh! Yeh!"
"Do you RE-PENT?"
"I repent!"
"AMEN! I REPENT!" Someone would yell and stretch out in the aisle and we'd giggle because we were teen-agers by now and liked fun. On Sundays about all we had to do was go to the Methodist church.
Sunday School. Morning service. Epworth League. Evening service.
Tan palmetto fans were spread in half-circles on the pews and in the sticky heat a lot of fanning went on. One time they had a revival for a week and we had to go every night. There was an "amen corner," with the women on one side and the men on the other. They sang so loud that we girls could talk and nobody could hear. But we kept our eye out for papa. When someone whispered, "Mr. Robinson's here," that was it—we were quiet!
Smith Carrington, a little carpenter we called "Uncle Smith," always wanted to preach and he walked up and down the street preaching to himself. One hot day a fat lady got to shouting and running up and down the aisle while everyone was singing. She grabbed Uncle Smith out of his pew, threw him down in the aisle and sat on him while we screamed with laughter.
Anyone who didn't belong to the church had to stand.
"All you sinners, stand!" the preacher yelled, and Bessie and I'd stand up along with the other sinners. **"Come up to the mourners' bench, sinners, and we will pray for your souls!"**
We'd traipse to the mourners' bench, kneel and bow our heads while all the saved came and prayed over us. I got so

tired of going to that mourners' bench, I joined the church when I was twelve and Bessie joined because I did.

One time a group of us was going to a Sunday School convention in a wagon, bouncing along on a country road in the woods. We bumped out of the woods and there were two white women in bonnets, plowing with mules.

"Lands a goshen!" the drive whispered.

All of us were looking at the women and it was so quiet you could have heard the earth turning under the plow if our wagon had stopped. It didn't! The driver shook the reins to shag us out of there!

"They's buck-naked!" someone said.

"Bare as new-hatched jaybirds!"

"Barer 'n baby possums!" We were all twittering.

"Quiet!" our driver hissed. "Quiet or I be swingin' from a rope!" He set that wagon jumping!

When we got home after the convention we told mama about the naked ladies in the field; everyone was talking about it.

"They musta done it on account of the heat," mama said. "Some folks can't stand the heat!"

THE TORNADO

I was home with mama and papa the Friday the tornado hit Washington in 1907. Jennie was across the hall waiting for friends to go to a church meeting and Minnie and Bessie had gone to sister's. Mozelle lived in a parsonage a block away because C. S. finally had a church.

All day it had thundered and the sky looked strange. Jennie said, "I wish it'd do what it's gonna do!"

I was in the bedroom with mama and papa. It was still and suddenly it sounded like a hundred trains. Wind wooshed in and doors banged shut. The kerosene lamp went out and the room was black. Then something lifted the house and shook it like a sifter. The beds, tables and chairs were sliding all over and I wondered if the world was ending. The roar changed to a hollow sound and debris was flying. I shut my eyes, felt more shaking and heard loud ripping above us, then felt cold air and rain.

24

Suddenly the roaring and shaking stopped. Mama and I were trembling from cold and we were soaked. I looked up and saw dark sky through a hole where the chimney had been. Then we heard the screaming.

Papa led us outside and we looked around and caught our breaths. Almost everything was gone or damaged! No houses near us were standing! Ours had been saved by two big trees that fell and held up the house, one from the front and one from the back. We hurried to the back yard and found the chickens buried in the roots of a fallen catalpa tree.

The screaming was coming from our Methodist church across the street: it had been flattened. Papa ran over and began bringing people home. Some had their legs broken. Some were bleeding. A lot of people came for the night and it was the first time I ever sat up all night.

An aristocratic widow, Mrs. Trimble, owned a boarding house and had a fat cook, Rose. The tornado tore up Rose's house and she was running around naked. "Miz Trimble! Miz Trimble!" Rose called, running to the boarding house. Someone grabbed a blanket and wrapped Rose.

An old retarded man named Billy was lifted and carried down to the bottomland. He came stumbling up the road hollering, "I'm dead! I'm dead!"

The black school was flattened, the Presbyterian church was moved into the street and many homes were demolished. All the outhouses were down and the men had to work fast to fix them!

Joe and Emma Green's granddaughter was blown away and her hip was broken. Later, she died. There was only one death the day of the tornado.

The Roystons had built a storm shelter in the safest place they had: under the brick carriage house. They had a servant girl they'd raised, Carrie Ship, who lived in the carriage house. Captain Charlie Royston found her buried in the storm shelter under a pile of bricks. At their main house, the kitchen and part of the home were torn off. Across the street from the Roystons' the front of the Aiken house stood but the kitchen was ripped away and the floor was torn up like matchsticks.

The pines that went down were twisted off and for miles and miles we could see sheets and clothing in the tops of pine trees. For weeks people came from all over to see the disaster at Washington. The government sent army tents for the homeless and gave us money for a new roof—about twenty dollars.

WORKING FOR ROYSTONS

Papa had a growin' thumb and years when we didn't have a tornado his garden looked as if it was laid out by an architect; he didn't let anybody in that garden until things were ready to pick. He grew everything, even tried to grow English walnuts.

Someone had a gristmill and we'd shuck and shell corn, then papa'd take it to the mill to be ground into cornmeal by a mule on a pole fastened to two big stones that went around. We didn't pay money—the owner took part of the cornmeal in exchange.

It was a good thing papa and mama were industrious and taught us to be proud of who we were because some things could have killed our spirit. Washington had plank walks in front of rich white people's homes but if a black person lived next door he had to walk in the mud.

There was a barbershop for blacks and one for whites. The barber for the white men was a black man, "Uncle Jim" Hamilton. He was the only Negro on the school board so he had status. Charlie Pettey was the barber for the black men in a little plank place with no sign.

A block up the street was the post office in a little house where everybody waited on the front porch for mail. We stood back so the white people could go first. The post office was run by Miss Rosie Wallace, a prim spinster who lived with her mother. Miss Rosie knew everybody, everybody knew her and she knew what was in their mail because she read it.

Next door to the Wallace's was the Royston mansion where I worked, taking slopjars to the outhouse to empty before and after school. When people came up the front steps past the tall columns of the home they entered a huge hall with an open staircase. On one side was a parlor with sliding doors and a dining room through another pair of sliding doors. To the rear, behind the kitchen was a room for the cook. The ceilings were high—ten feet or so—and upstairs the front bedrooms had french doors onto a balcony that went the length of the house across a veranda. The hall, staircase and parlor had carpets and the bedroom furniture gleamed—poster beds, red mahogany furniture and rosewood dressers with marble tops.

Mrs. Molly Royston was a white-haired old lady who prayed a lot. Her husband, Charles, had been in the army and everyone called him "Captain Royston." The Aikins lived across the street in a nice house and Roystons socialized a little with them, but few families were the Roystons' social equals because most of the aristocracy had died or moved away.

Three grown daughters lived with Miss Molly and the Captain in the summer: Miss Mattie, Miss Bessie and Miss Irene. Miss Irene taught in Prescott and stayed with her parents when school was out; her parents still called her "little Irene." Miss Stella was married to a judge, Miss Lena had married a farmer and Miss Bessie had married Mr. Battle. They had a home in Fulton, but she was at her parents' all the time so her husband came to visit on week-ends. The Roystons' son, Grandison, was in college and later became a well-known doctor in St. Louis. He was the handsomest man I ever saw!

Miss Mattie taught school for the blind in Little Rock, then lost her hearing and became a teacher for the deaf. She had such an influence on my life! She was precise and when I did anything that wasn't right she'd make me do it over. To this day I have to do things the right way. It was Miss Mattie who changed my name from "Regina" to "Reginald." I never liked the way people pronounced "Rag-nah," so one day Mattie said, "Why don't you change your name to 'Reginald'?" And I did. I began signing my name that way and I asked people to call me Reginald.

Miss Mattie wrote a lot of letters and she'd wait until I was ready to go home in the afternoon, then ask me to take them to the post office. I was afraid to go when a lot of people were on the post office porch and Miss Mattie knew it. But when Miss Irene was home she'd sneak me out before Miss Mattie could catch me. "Run, Reg, run!" Miss Irene would call.

Every morning Miss Molly went into the parlor, closed the sliding doors and sat in the dark praying and meditating. They

kept it dark in the parlor and dining room and never opened
the shutters unless company came. When Miss Molly was
praying for her children, Miss Bessie'd call, "Give a good one
for me, Mother!"

THE DAVIS HOUSE

Russell and Miami Davis owned a fine hotel for white
people, the Davis House, and you couldn't tell Mr. Davis from
a white man, but he'd been a slave. Miami Davis'
mother—Richard Samuels' widow—lived with them, but she was
elderly and never went out.

The Davis House was famous for its food and when court
was held twice a year, all the lawyers stayed there, but
famous speakers and politicans usually stayed in Hope. The
only other lodging was the Petty House, a small hotel for
Negroes, but it didn't do much business because most black
people stayed with relatives if they visited, and speakers like
Booker T. Washington stayed in Hope.

Russell and Miami had a big staff and did well financially.
Mr. Davis couldn't read or write and papa had to write his
letters and do his books for him. The Davis House was doing
fine when Mr. and Mrs. Black built a hotel across from them;
then the white people began going to the Blacks' hotel and
the Davis House began going down. I don't know if that was
the cause of it, but afterwards Miami Davis began to lose her
mind. She'd been a fine lady but she was never mentally right
again.

Russell Davis was still holding onto the business when a
black preacher, Reverend Rufus Stout, came to Washington.
He wanted to build a new railroad because the only train that
came through had about two cars and made a round trip from
Hope to Nashville, Arkansas, everyday. Stout wanted to start
a train in Washington that would run in the other direction to
rural towns that had no railroad—like Columbus, Saratoga and
Macedonia—where there was a lot of cotton to be hauled. So
he formed a company and Russell Davis became president.
The people thought building the railroad was a good idea and
almost everyone bought a few shares or stocks, including
plantation owners in the little towns. Including papa. Including
Russell Davis.

Papa could see by the account books that Mr. Davis was investing heavily in the railroad and he was worried about it, but it looked like the railroad was coming and everyone would be rich because surveyors were working and men were digging the roadbed. Then it all fell through. The tracks were never laid and Russell Davis lost all of his money.

But Reverend Stout didn't give up. He had a good mind and brought electricity to town; a black electrician, Mose Betton, put in the first electric lights. You might say that Stout and Betton lit up the town.

4
Learning and Lynchings

As I grew into my teens I discovered that young minority women either had to work in white kitchens or teach school. Other than marriage, those were our career choices. Papa never would let us work in a kitchen.

"Papa, why can't I get a kitchen job?" I pleaded. "It pays more'n emptying slopjars—Manda Lee works in a kitchen!"

"Her folks don't give a hoot or a howl about anything!" papa said, clenching his jaw. "I don't want to hear another word!"

The subject was dropped, but I couldn't understand why papa was so against my cooking until mama told me.

"It's a rough thing to say, but some men's bad about molestin' servant girls—that's how we got so many shades of tan. All's you got to do is look in the mirror. 'Member your great-grandma Becky?" I nodded. "She could prob'ly have told you all about kitchens!" mama said. "Don't know as that's where Dr. W. caught up with her, but it's likely his attentions could've started over a hot stove!"

Great-grandma Becky . . . So that was why papa put his foot down! Late that night I was still thinking about what mama had told me. It set me to thinking about other things papa was strong against, like Harriet.* Big Harriet was a loose single woman who had a child and lived in a house with two other women. One day I'd been at the post office waiting to mail letters, when I noticed that most of the men on the porch were smiling secret-like and gazing across the street. So I looked, too.

Harriet and two women were walking slowly, swaying, smiling and glancing at the men. I couldn't figure out why the

30

men were smirking. And why were the ladies on the porch turning their backs to the street and fanning fast with their letters? They'd been talking like there was no tomorrow until they saw Harriet. Then they got quiet and glanced at each other out of the corners of their eyes with their eyebrows up like they knew a secret. It was a secret to me, that was sure, until mama told me why papa was against kitchen work.

One night that same summer, papa stomped up the steps and into the kitchen and I ran to open the bedroom door a crack so I could hear. Papa was usually quiet, so I knew that when he banged the door something was up.

"Danged Harriet's put her hooks into young Joe Smith!"* papa said, banging his fist on the table.

"Poor Frank and Addie!"* mama said, sounding as if she'd cry. She and papa were close friends of Smiths.

"Only one way to handle that woman!" papa said. "We don't need the likes of her in this town!" He hurried out the back door and mama slumped onto a chair.

Papa didn't harm Harriet. He couldn't harm my pet pig, let alone a human being—not even one the likes of Harriet. No, papa just ran her out of town.

"Said she's gonna get even," he told mama later. "Had an evil look in her eye. The woman's up to no good!"

A few weeks later we found out what big Harriet was up to: she got young Joe to marry her. From that day on, his life went downhill. Harriet and Joe lived in a little shack in the country near Washington and sharecropped. Maybe having Harriet for a wife and the sharecropping life were too much for Joe or maybe he'd have lost his mind anyway. There was a streak of insanity on his mother's side passed on by the men—it always struck the oldest son.

"Joe Smith gettin' lak a chil'," Aunt Mary B. said. Mama was snapping beans on the front porch and Mary came up and lowered herself stiffly onto the porch swing.

"You don't say!" mama snapped the words with the beans. "When'd you see Joe Smith?"

"Yestiday. Seed 'im when I be strollin'."

"In the country?"

Aunt Mary nodded and gave a toothless grin. "Be strollin' right pas' they place!"

"Aunt Mary, you gonna keel over, you keep strollin' three miles outa town!" Mama didn't sound worried about the

31

possibility and the beans were flying into the pan.

"Plumb los' track o' my tracks," Aunt Mary said. "Fust thing I knowed, I be askin' fo' a drink a water at Joe's door an'—God rest my soul if I ain't tellin' the trute!—Joe comes ta da door and don' know ol' Aunt Mary!"

Mama stopped and stared at Mary.

"They say he does anything Harriet wants him to," mama said. Aunt Mary nodded so that the flower on her straw hat bobbed.

"Yea! Yea! That be fact so far as he's able ta carry out what she wants! That woman plumb broke 'im! She's strong 's a ox, don't hoe or chop cotton like other women—plows the field."

A few months later, Harriet left her field work for a few days when she gave birth to a baby girl. Less than two years passed when Aunt Mary brought another report. "Harriet's tied up with another man," she said. "So far along, 'pears she done swallow a watermelon seed!"

It became common knowledge that Harriet had a man living in the shack with her and Joe. Frank Smith told papa that his son's mind was so wrecked, he slept on a pallet on the floor while this man and Harriet slept in his bed. By and by Harriet had three babies by the man. Still, Joe stayed and wouldn't let anyone say a word against her. And she watched out for him, treated him like he was her child. Finally he got some sense, broke away and went to live with his parents. Years later his real daughter had a son who became mentally unbalanced. He was the oldest son.

FRIENDS AND THE POORHOUSE

Bessie, Minnie and I went around with Claudie and Willie Shepperson. Their father, Archie Shepperson, was the first minority teacher and principal in Washington and Hempstead County. Mr. and Mrs. Shepperson were both very light; it wasn't right, but we had a caste system and certain ones ran together. We went to church and did everything with the Shepperson girls.

Faye Dangerfield was another friend—we'd known each other since we were babies and I have memories of pulling her hair while we were in our mothers' arms. Her mother, Lilly, was a widow and she and mama were friends. Lilly had rheumatism and couldn't walk, just sat in a chair all the time.

"Lilly, I'm gonna make you walk!" I said one day.

"Anyone can make these legs churn's sent by the Lord!" she said.

"Just put your arm around my neck," I said and with my arm around her waist, we began walking back and forth. I worked with her for weeks and she eventually walked with a cane. She loved me for that and she never forgot me.

Somehow I'd learned to care about older people even though I'd done something in my childhood that I wasn't proud of. It was hard to find excitement when I was young and sometimes my friends and I'd be sitting on the front steps, saying how bored we were.

"Why don't we go to the poorhouse?" somebody'd say.

"Yeh! Why don't we?"

And off we'd run, beating it down the road toward Columbus and the small frame poorhouse. No one was ever around to stop us, so we'd walk in and stand for a minute to let our eyes adjust to the dark hallway running the length of the building.

Moans, screams and wild jabbering echoed, and along the hall hands reached out from between bars in small openings of heavy doors. It smelled worse than an outhouse and I gagged. As if our inner clocks had been set together, suddenly we all tore down the hall. My chest felt like a hot potato about to burst as we raced through the stench, between screams and groping hands. On we ran, past the cell where a naked man lay in dirty straw, out into sun and sweet air. Gasping and inhaling smells of freshly cut hay, we laughed giddily, celebrating our freedom. We'd imagined the people were trying to grab us. Now that I'm older than most of them were, I've wondered: Did they only want a gentle touch?

Poorhouse adventures were behind us in our middle teens when we went on picnics, to church and literary society meetings. All of us had beaus, but we girls would walk together while the boys strolled behind us.

And we went horseback riding. Most of the boys came from

farms and each one had to furnish a horse for his girl, so he had to have two horses and saddles. The young people met at our house because mama was easy-going, and there'd be a crowd and lots of horses in front of the house. Once I was having the biggest time on a frisky horse and laughing as we galloped through town. I didn't know the horse was running away until they told me later!

"If you don't run after boys, they'll run after you," mama taught us, so I let the boys do the running. I'd always been friends with Tim Follett,* and we called ourselves twins because our mothers were friends and we were both born on September 20. I took it for granted Tim and I would marry some day. He lived in the nearby town of Follett,* named for his family. Few people had cars, but Tim had one; all three boys in his family did. They were well-to-do because their family owned a store and ran the post office.

I was sixteen, so it must have been 1910 when there was a meeting at Follett and Nona Berry said, "Let's drive up there." Nona Vaultz Berry was a gifted pianist and the young music teacher at Haygood. She was married, but not much older than we were. She'd been engaged to my cousin, Noble, before I knew her—that was Aunt Minnie's son. Then a crazy guy in Little Rock had stabbed him to death. It just about killed Nona, too, she'd been so in love. I hadn't known her then but she'd become a good friend and when she wanted to go to Follett, I was ready.

"Let's!" I said. "Won't Tim be surprised?"

So Nona and I rented a horse and buggy and wheeled up to Follett. We stopped to talk to friends on the dirt main street and it was then that I saw Tim ambling down the street with Sally May from Ashdown hanging on him.

"Nona, let's get out of here!" I whispered.

She looked up and saw Tim, and at the same time he saw us. Then he tried to slip his arm from Sally May, but she'd seen me and there wasn't any breaking her grip on Tim Follett. She was about to drag him over to us when Nona shook the reins and wheeled the buggy back toward home. When we got home I ran to my room. That week I got a letter from Tim saying he was coming to talk on Sunday.

"Tim's going to be here Sunday, but I'm not!" I told mama.

"You never not been where Tim wanted to be since you was babies," mama said.

"Appears he wants to be where Sally May is now!" I said and mama raised her eyebrows in her "ah ha!" look. She stopped mixing the cornmeal, came and put her arm around me.

"'Pears a green-eyed monster's run the snakes out," she said gently.

"Biggest snake-in-the-grass is at Follett!" I said and buried my face against her shoulder.

"Don't take it so to heart," she said softly. "Reckon you're all mixed up 'cause Tim's been like a brother since you took your first breath."

"I reckon so!" I cried. Then I ran out the door and stumbled through the fields to the woods. When things closed in I walked in the woods until the trees and earth healed me. This time they didn't heal.

When Sunday came I said I was going to Faye's for the day and asked mama not to tell Tim where I was. I never did forgive Tim until years later and that was mean of me. I was quick with the temper and I haven't lost all of it yet.

The same year I lost Tim, I lost my sister Minnie—she got married. I was her maid of honor, and I cried on her wedding day: July 4, 1910. I remember, it was the same day that Jack Johnson became the first black man to win the world boxing championship.

Minnie was supposed to get married on Sunday but her fiance, William Arthur Morrow (we called him "W. A.") missed the train in Brinkley, so they had to get married on Monday. It was a long wait, but all the people came back to the Methodist church for the wedding. The Royston sisters had done all the decorating, had even made a bell-shaped umbrella out of cedar for Minnie and William to stand under. Miss Molly was sick and couldn't come, but the rest of the Roystons were there.

Among the black people, most preachers were teachers, and W. A. was a preacher and teacher in Marvel. Minnie was a teacher, too, but it wasn't long before she had a family to raise—eventually they had nine children.

So my sister was gone but I wasn't about to get married. I was in the last class to graduate from the original Haygood Seminary, then I was offered a job teaching first grade there. I had a good memory and was salutatorian of the class—and I'd helped the valedictorian with her work! Jennie had

Haygood Methodist Seminary

completed Haygood's millinery course and Mozelle, Minnie, Bessie and I became teachers.

By that time Professor Matthew Mark Wilbun, one of our former teachers, had succeeded Professor Tyus as president of Haygood and had married one of my best friends, Claudia Shepperson, so I was very close to both of them. (A lot of people spelled his name "Wilburn," with an "r," but after he moved we corresponded for years and he always signed his name "Matthew Wilbun.")

Mr. Wilbun's story was remarkable because his father was an itinerate preacher who didn't believe in school, so Matthew had been self-taught and hadn't put his foot in a school until he was nineteen. Once he started his formal education he didn't stop until he had degrees from two colleges—Paine College in Augusta, Georgia, and Lane College in Jackson, Tennessee. Later, he became a professor at Philander Smith College in Little Rock. He and I discussed books for hours, and one year he gave me THE RUBAIYAT by Omar Khayyam, the Persian poet and astronomer.

ARSON AT HAYGOOD SEMINARY

I'd just begun teaching first grade at Haygood Seminary when the tragedy struck. One morning just as I was waking up mama rushed into my room.

"You don't have to go to school today, honey—Haygood's gone, burned down," she said sadly.

I let out a cry and sank onto the bed. There was no fire department in Washington. Anything that burned went to the ground.

"It burned last night," mama said, smoothing my hair. "All the buildings is gone."

"Was—was anybody killed?" I asked.

"No, praise the Lord!" mama said. "They all got out. Said everything went up in flames at once. Your papa says it was probably arson."

"The buildings were spread out," I said dully, thinking of the old mansion they'd converted into an administration building. Tyus Hall, the new dormitory for girls. The chapel in the boys' building. The primary building. The high school.

They all burned to the ground. So Haygood was moved to Pine Bluff and became affiliated with the state school system.

After the fire, I went to Texas College near Dallas for nearly a year to study home economics. Professor Tyus had become president there and Nona Berry was teaching music, and she persuaded me to come. She and I shared a dormitory room and once she told an amazing story about losing a diamond ring.

"There's this island off the coast of Louisiana where Cajuns live, and an old black woman named Aunt Lucy lives there," she said. "People told me she'd know where my ring was because she knew and could see things that we couldn't. I didn't believe it, but there was no harm in trying so I went down to the island and when I went into Aunt Lucy's house she said, 'Sit down. Your train don't leave 'til five o'clock.' There were a lot of people in the room—people came from all over to see her—and I had to wait my turn. Aunt Lucy told me that the ring was stolen and who took it. Back home I confronted the thief and he gave the ring back."

At the end of the school year in Texas I got my first teaching assignment since Haygood, at a dot on the map called "Blackbottom." My brother-in-law, William Morrow, taught in Marvel and was county examiner for Negro teachers. He told me they needed a teacher at Blackbottom, so I applied and got the job. It was the first of several country schools I taught in over the next ten years.

I stayed with Minnie and W. A. on week-ends because Marvel was closer than Washington. During the week I boarded with a family, and on Friday afternoons Monroe picked me up with his fine horse and buggy to take me to Minnie's.

Monroe was a short, plump young man who took me to socials. He came from a nice family and carried mail in the country, so he had a good job and was a sharp dresser. But what impressed me most was his running account at the ice cream parlor in Marvel. I could go there with my friends, eat as much ice cream as we wanted and charge it to Monroe! Then Monroe spoiled it by getting serious and at the end of the school year he asked me to marry him. I said "No," that I had no intention of getting married, then I went home and forgot him.

Once in awhile I'd go to Texarkana to visit Bessie. She'd married James Douglas who was almost twenty years older and had become a friend of George Washington Carver at Tuskegee Institute in Alabama. Booker T. Washington believed in technical training and James graduated in bricklaying but became a railroad mail clerk. James and George Washington Carver corresponded, and Carver visited them in Texarkana.

IN HOT WATER IN HOT SPRINGS

In summer I'd visit Faye and Lilly in Hot Springs, where they'd moved. It was a delightful place, with houses built up in the hills, ostrich racing on Whittington Avenue and tourists coming to Bathhouse Row.

Lilly's sister, Ada, was the pantrywoman at the Majestic Hotel and made good money, so she owned rental property and let Lilly and Faye live in a house next to hers on Pine Street, two or three blocks from the hotel.

After Ada got too old to be pantrywoman, the manager

gave her a lifetime job as nursemaid to his boy and let her do a little work around the hotel. Faye cooked for people and was Lilly's sole support. I'd visit with Lilly and when Faye came home in the afternoon, we'd dress up and go out on Whittington Avenue to buy an ice cream. There was one free spring left.

"Don't you take Reg down and give her none of that water!" Lilly warned Faye.

"Why'd you think I'd do that?" Faye said innocently.

And the first chance she got, Faye took me down for a drink. "Gotta taste this water, Reg," she said. "Purer than the spring back home!"

Faye being a prankster, I should have known better, but it was hot and I was thirsty so I started drinking and didn't stop until I'd quenched my thirst. We began walking and suddenly I knew if I didn't run I wouldn't make it home in time. I took off running, with Faye behind me, laughing. The water was a laxative! She got a kick out of that, but not as much as I did.

LYNCHINGS

After the railroad came to Hope, the county seat was moved there and then they kept shuffling records between the towns. That was funny! Papa, attorney Luke Monroe, and Will Etter from the paper would go to Hope for records and bring them to Washington, then someone from Hope would come and take them back.

Each summer, teachers took a two or three week course at the Normal School in Hope. I'd walk carefully there because it was different than Washington and I was afraid. Negroes lived in a separate section, and I remembered something that had happened a few years earlier.

The road to Hope ran right by our house and one night we'd heard cars slowly rolling past. The drivers didn't want to wake up the people, but we were awake because papa knew trouble was coming and had gone downtown. He was probably in the thick of things when the mob forced its way into the jail for a black prisoner and pushed him into one of the cars. Mama, Jennie, Minnie, Bessie and I watched from behind the curtains as the cars went by. By the light of the moon we could see shotguns sticking up out of the cars. They took the man towards Hope and lynched him.

Another time, there was a mud puddle on a boardwalk and a black man met a white woman on the walk. She claimed he grabbed her, but he said she slipped and was falling off the walk and he caught her. Anyway, a mob lynched him.

Once a train called "The Sunset Limited" came by when a guy was hanging from a telegraph pole near the depot. It upset a white woman in a pullman so, she made a fuss and I don't think they hung anyone from telegraph poles after that.

5

Courtship
by Correspondence

"Willard Heard's one of the nicest people I know, Reg," Jenny Sanford said.

"Maybe, but everyone says he's bashful," I said. Jenny was trying to fix up a long distance romance and I wasn't interested. I'd met Jenny when we were in college in Texas. Now it was the summer of 1918 and I was visiting her at her home in Evanston, Illinois, where she lived with her husband and mother. We were barefoot, kicking along, sifting sand through our toes on a beach by Lake Michigan. Jenny told me that her mother and Willard Heard's mother had been friends in Milwaukee for years.

"Willard and I were like brother and sister," she said.

"I had a friend like that once," I said, picking up a flat stone and hurling it sidearm into the water. It plopped. I tried another one and it bounced lightly, dancing on the sun in the water. "One, two, three—FOUR!" I shrieked and we raced to skip them, laughed and threw more. When we were tired of that, we gathered up our long skirts to hold shells and stones.

Later in the day, the rocks were in small piles on the porch and we were doing dishes in the kitchen when Jenny began talking about Willard Heard again.

"Did I tell you that he sings?" she said.

"What's he sing?" I asked casually. "Better do this fork over." I slipped it back into her dishpan and fished two spoons out of the rinse water.

"Tenor, I think," Jenny said, and poked between the fork tines with a knife. "Mama said he could be an actor, but you know how that goes. He's almost as light as you, but he's tan enough so the world isn't a stage for him!"

"It isn't exactly a stage for me, either," I said, "but I've met some bad actors!" We both laughed and dumped the water in the sink.

"Why don't you write to him?" Jenny persisted. We were taking off our aprons and walking out to sit on the front porch with her mother.

"Seems to me the man should write first," I said and sat on the swing. Jenny's mother nodded in agreement.

"It's too bad he's so shy," she said.

"Well, if this Willard wants a pen pal," I said, "he's going to have to start the writing!"

A few days later, I went back to Arkansas and forgot about Willard Heard. Then one day a letter came from him. Jenny had given him my address, he said. Would I like to correspond with him? I answered his letter and soon we were writing regularly.

We were still writing the next year when I was teaching in Texarkana, where I stayed with Bessie and James. Bessie had heard that there were some vacancies in the school district, so we went over to the school board office. Our hearts sank when we saw an old white man at the main desk. We told him why we were there and he asked for our names. Bessie told him and the old man peered at us.

"I don't know but one Robinson in Washington!" he said. "Y'all kin to Nobie Robinson?"

"He's our father," Bessie said.

"Y'all are Nobie's children?" he grinned. "My name's Captain Stuart! I've known Nobie Robinson most of my life and it'd be my privilege to hire his daughters!" So we were soon teaching.

Bessie and I were different. She liked clothes, knitting and handwork, but she didn't care much about books. James and I liked to read, and he'd find articles for Bessie.

"Look at this and tell me what it's about," she'd say after he left the house, "so when he asks me, I can tell him what it's about!" It was our secret joke: I'd fill her in so she could discuss articles with her husband.

One of my friends had a sister, Piranda, who lived in Hope. Her husband, Ralph, got a job in Milwaukee, so Piranda went to Milwaukee and they met Willard through Jenny Sanford. Then Piranda began pestering me, wanting me to meet Willard. Finally in 1920 Jenny arranged for Willard and me to meet at her house in Evanston during summer vacation; we'd been corresponding for almost two years. Jenny and I were in the living room when someone knocked on the door and she went to see who it was.

"Willard!" she said. "Whatever are you doing here?"

My heart jumped when I heard her say his name, but I didn't even have time to straighten my dress. In walked a handsome young man with the kindest smile I'd ever seen, except maybe for mama.

"I knew you were the one the minute I saw you in Jenny's living room!" he told me later. Much later. At first he was shy, but we went walking and began visiting.

"You have a dream?" I asked. I knew that Willard had worked as a host at The Surf restaurant and for wealthy white families in Milwaukee.

"A dream?" he said.

"Isn't there something you'd like to do, something you'd be happy doing all your life?"

"Sing, I guess. I like to sing," he said. "But they're not looking for tan singers in Milwaukee," he said and glanced at me as we walked toward the lake. "How about you? You got a dream?"

"I'd almost forgotten," I said. "It probably sounds silly, but my mother used to get magazines and I'd look at the ads for fine china and silver and think it'd be grand to have a teashop!" I paused and laughed. "Not much need for a country schoolteacher to be carrying around an uppity dream like that!"

"Sounds like a fine one to me," Willard said. Then he looked at his feet and mumbled, "Maybe you won't always be a country schoolteacher."

He kept staring at his feet and we walked a long time. Later, after dinner, we decided to keep writing to each other; then he left to catch his train.

LITTLE ROCK: PATTERSON'S GROCERY STORE

That summer, I went to Little Rock to stay with Uncle Ernest and Aunt Mag because Uncle Ernest got me a job at Patterson's Grocery Store there. It was a nice place to work and a lot of wealthy black people shopped there.

Aunt Mag was a woman who'd had a mishap and had a baby out of wedlock, and grandma and them never forgave her, treated her like an outcast. But Uncle Ernest had two children by her: Jason was at Philander Smith College and their youngest son, Monroe, had died. Mag's son, Amon, was grown but no one said where he was, if they knew.

Uncle Ernest was mama's brother and he got me the job at the grocery store because he knew the owner, Mr. Patterson. Bessie and I always laughed that Uncle Ernest managed to go with the best people wherever he was, even at the state capitol where he was a janitor. My uncle was so good to me, he didn't want to charge board and there I was, making a lot of money—sixteen dollars a week!

I was just about running Patterson's by myself because Mr. Patterson had lost his job with the railroad and that pretty near killed him. I don't know where he was, but he was hardly ever around that store. Arkansas was a dry state from the time I can remember—they'd voted liquor out for ninety-nine years—and Mr. Patterson let someone talk him into smuggling liquor down on a railroad car. My brother-in-law, James, was a railroad mail clerk and he knew all about liquor smuggling. He said there were always government investigators on the trains.

"This is my last trip," Mr. Patterson had said. "I ain't gonna haul liquor no more!"

And they caught him. He must have been getting it from St. Louis on the way to New Orleans. I don't think he got sent to prison, but the railroad fired him. He let me run the store and I enjoyed visiting with the customers. Among them was Professor Matthew Wilbun. He and Claudie lived in Little Rock because Matthew taught at Shorter College across the river during the school term. In summer, he worked on the railroad. Professor Wilbun never considered himself too good for any kind of work.

One day, who strolled into the store but my old boyfriend, Monroe!

"Hello, Regie. I've been looking for you," he said.

I was polishing the glass on the candy counter and when I heard his voice I almost dropped my rag.

"Hello, Monroe," I said and kept wiping.

"Regie, I'd like to talk," he said.

"I'm listenin'," I said, and the next thing I knew, he was

proposing, asking me to marry him again. I'm ashamed to say it—and in recent years I've thought back on that day and asked the Lord to forgive me—but I wasn't very nice to him. I was cool, didn't hardly speak, and finally he left.

A few weeks later I heard he was dead. I've always wondered how he died and if the way I treated him had anything to do with it. He might have been dying anyhow, but I've always wondered.

ENGAGEMENTS: WILLARD, AND WHELEN SPRINGS

One of the biggest mistakes I ever made was leaving Little Rock to teach at a place called Whelen Springs. Mr. Patterson offered me inducements to stay, but I decided to go to Whelen Springs. At the end of summer I went to Washington to stay until I could start my new assignment. Black children only went to school five months a year—a two-month summer term and a three-month winter term—because they had to work in the cotton fields.

So I was living at home when the letter from Willard came. My mouth must've fallen open when I began to read.

"What's the matter?" mama asked.

"He wants me to marry him," I whispered. "Willard Heard wants me to marry him!" I turned to a second page. It was a letter from Octavia Williams, Willard's mother, saying that she would welcome me into the family.

"You rather be a old maid?" mama asked.

"I don't know," I said, folding the letters and slipping them back in the envelope. "I've only met him once..."

"You been writin' long 'nough!"

"Writin' isn't the same as bein' with!" I walked to my bedroom, sank onto the bed and stared at the ceiling. That night I went to sleep trying to quiet questions turning in my mind like the stone at the gristmill.

A few days later, mama and papa got a letter from Willard asking for my hand in marriage.

"I don't have no objection," papa said. "You're twenty-six, getting to be an old maid!"

Old maid. There it was again. If a young woman passed twenty without a ring on her finger, people began to label her. Most of my friends had married and moved away and Willard's letter came at the right time. "He's a good person—handsome, too," I said to myself. Finally I wrote and accepted his proposal. A few weeks later a beautiful diamond ring came in the mail: I was engaged!

Then Willard wanted to get married right away, but I wanted to teach one more time to earn money to buy clothes. I'd always let everybody use my money, mainly mama and papa. I didn't do much for myself—I was always trying to help somebody else. So now I wanted some new clothes, like every bride. Willard insisted that we marry sooner and wrote: "Don't worry about clothes. You come North and I'll buy you all the clothes you need." I answered that I wanted to teach one more time. After I moved to Milwaukee, I knew I wouldn't be able to because I wasn't accredited and I wasn't white.

So that winter I went to Whelen Springs. The settlement was in a wild part of Arkansas and all eight grades were in a one-room school. Some of the boys were as big as men and because I was young they wouldn't obey, just laughed at me. One day I got tired of it and sent the two big Jackson* brothers home. The students began to snicker and whisper and soon the room was buzzing.

"Miz Jackson gwanna whip Miz Robinson!"

"Miz Robinson oughta seen what happen ta da las' teacher!"

"Miz Robinson too l'il ta fight a flea!"

Those children had me shaking, but I kept teaching.

A little later, I looked out the door and here comes this great big scowling woman with a bandana tied on her head. I didn't know whether she could read or not, but when she got to the school I showed her to a seat and gave her a book, then I gave the kids recess.

"Miz Robinson, why yo' sen' ma boys home?" she boomed when they'd gone outside.

"They weren't obeying," I said, "and I couldn't do anything with them."

"Ah sen' ma boys ta school ta get a edjacashun and I DON' WAN' 'EM TA BE SENT HOME!" she yelled. Then she lowered her voice, leaned forward and almost smiled. "Any time yo' can't handle 'em, yo' sen' fo' me—ah'll take care of 'em!" She whirled around and left.

It was pretty rough in that area. The houses were shacks and I had to live in the cabin of the member of the school board who hired me. They paid me fifty dollars a month to teach and the community was supposed to make it ten dollars extra, but they never paid me a penny. And I had to pay twenty dollars for my board! It looked like it was going to take a long time to buy clothes for my marriage.

I had a bare room with a bed and a cornshuck mattress in the shack where the board member and his peculiar wife from Louisiana lived. Shortly after I came, I mentioned that I liked turnip greens and cornbread. The woman sent me dinner—turnip greens and cornbread every noon, great big dishes that were hot when they got there. I had them morning, noon and night! Sometimes there might be ham hocks, but I had greens and cornbread three times a day all the while I was there. I was so thankful when the term ended, I began to welcome the thought of marriage.

A DAY LATE FOR MY WEDDING

What little money I made, I saved and managed to buy some clothes by spring. Willard and I had decided to be married on April 29, 1921, at Jenny Sanford's in Evanston. Then we'd go to a reception at Willard's mother's house in Milwaukee.

Willard made all the plans so everything would go smoothly. He even had our announcements printed and sent to me. He'd grown up under the name of "Kinner," his first stepfather. He told his mother he didn't want to be married under that name because Kinner hadn't adopted him, so he took his real name, "Heard." He hardly remembered his father because he'd died in Alabama when Willard was young. So our name was "Heard" on the announcements I left with mama and papa.

"Don't send them out until a week after I'm gone," I told them. I wanted to be married and in Milwaukee before anyone knew about it. It was spring and everything was green and in bloom and I wondered if I was doing the right thing. Was it possible? I was marrying a man I'd only met once!

The train didn't stop in little places like Hope, so I told mama and papa "Good-by," and went to Texarkana and stayed with Bessie before I left for the North. I'd written to Willie Shepperson in St. Louis and she wrote that her husband would meet me at the station there; I'd have time for a visit with

Willie before I caught the train to Chicago, where Willard and his mother would meet me. The three of us would go to Evanston together.

The Sunshine Special ran from Texarkana to St. Louis, but there was no sun when I left. It was a stormy night on April 28 when James took me to the station. We sat on a bench under the depot roof to stay out of the rain, and it was thundering and lightening all around. We saw the train's light before we heard the engine. James waved and ran alongside it, but it just whizzed on past. In about an hour we saw another train coming, but it wasn't slowing down, either.

"Come on!" James yelled. "We're getting you on this train!" We ran out into the storm and raced beside the train with James yelling to the conductor and me. **"Grab his hand!"** he yelled over the thunder. I was scared, but I ran and reached for the conductor's hand. Suddenly he clasped my wrist, I grabbed hold and he hauled me onto the train.

"All 'board, li'l Miss!" he said. I thanked him and lurched along the swaying aisle until I found an empty seat. The conductor brought the suitcase James had thrown on after me, and I took off my coat and got settled.

Miles went by, then some waiters and pullmen came and tried to get me to go back in the coach where they were having drinks. I told them I was getting married, and had sense enough not to go. Finally, we got to St. Louis and Willie Shepperson's chauffeur husband met me at the station with a big car and took me to their place. Willie and I hadn't seen each other for years and we threw our arms around each other when I got to their apartment. It was crowded because Willie had invited friends in to meet me, and everyone was talking at once.

"We never thought you'd make it, Reg!" Willie said. "There's a new hotel opening downtown and we'd like to have a party for you."

"That's nice," I said, "but I don't know—I should rest before I catch my train." That night I was to catch the train to Chicago.

"Aw, c'mon! It's once in a lifetime!" Willie's husband said. "Don't worry—I'll get you to your train on time!"

It didn't take much convincing after that. I loved to dance and we didn't have parties in Washington. And I sure hadn't been to any in Whelen Springs! Besides, they were having it for me. I changed into one of my new dresses and we went to this grand new hotel with chandeliers and all, and soon I was dancing and having a big time with everyone telling me how light I was on my feet. I even had a sip of champagne. The hours passed and then Willie's husband and another friend who was a chauffeur were arguing over who was going to take me to the station. Finally, Willie's husband drove me and we pulled up to the depot just after the train for Chicago had pulled out!

"Oh, Reg, I'm sorry!" Willie said when we got back to the apartment.

"Not as sorry as I am," I said.

I was upset, but people were always missing trains because they weren't on schedule, so we went back to the apartment and Willie sent a telegram to Milwaukee. I hoped Willard hadn't left for Chicago yet. If he had, his stepfather would tell the people coming to our wedding dinner that we'd be late. And Willard would have a long wait in Chicago.

WEDDING IN WAUKEGAN

Late the next afternoon, Willard looked worried when he reached up to help me off the train.

"These trains! Either early or late!" I said.

"I'm glad you made it," Willard said nervously, and introduced me to his mother. Octavia hugged me and smiled the same gentle smile that Willard had.

"My, oh, my!" she said. "You were right, Willard—she was worth waiting for!"

"Mom and I were in Evanston when Robert wired us that you'd missed your train," Willard said. "It's too late to go back there—we'd miss the train to Milwaukee."

"What about Jenny?" I said.

"She understands—said to send her love," Willard said. "I checked on Waukegan, and if we catch the next train we can make it to the Justice of the Peace and get to Milwaukee tonight."

I was ashamed that I'd spoiled our plans—and Jenny Sanford's. Later, Willard told me that he wondered if I'd stood him up. Ours wasn't one of those passionate affairs everyone dreams about, but we were both ready to get married and try to make a good life together. We caught the train to Waukegan, found the Justice of the Peace and stood with Octavia behind us as he read from a book. It was April 30, 1921.

"Do you, Regina, take this man, Willard, to be your lawfully wedded husband...?" I was scared to death as we said our vows!

6

Marriage and Milwaukee

After the ceremony, we caught a train to Milwaukee. As I'd traveled north, I'd noticed that there weren't as many flowers blooming as there were in Arkansas, but there was still a lot of green in Missouri. The land was flatter through Illinois, with less flowers and leaves. When we came to Wisconsin, it was night and I couldn't see anything from the window of the train.

In Milwaukee, Willard's step-uncle met us at the station with a Pierce-Arrow: Hollis Kinner drove for a rich white family. The Kinner's had been one of the first Negro families in the city. And didn't Hollis want to drive all over and show me the town, tired as I was! Up and down the streets we went, with Hollis pointing to things, and me not caring but trying to be polite. The trees looked bare by the light of the gas lamps and it seemed like hours before we pulled up in front of a big brick duplex.

"Here we are!" Willard said.

Numbly, I climbed from the car and Willard slipped his hand under my arm. We climbed some stairs to a porch and he opened the door. I could hear voices as we climbed the stairs to the Williams'—and our—second floor flat. Someone opened the door, and there were all the people.

"They're here!" someone called.

"You been missing a nice party!"

"Hush! Can't you see she's tired?"

"You must be Reginald!"

Most seemed happy but they'd been waiting all day and some of them looked disgusted.

"So this is Reginald!" a tall man said and took my arm.

"I'm Robert Williams. Guess that makes me your new father!"

Suddenly everybody was talking and making introductions, and someone led us to the dining room to see the table that Mrs. Kelly had prepared. She was head cook at The Surf and rented a room in the attic above Octavia and Robert. Mrs. Kelly had cooked a lovely dinner, but I was too upset to eat. Finally, after what seemed like forever, the guests left and we all went to bed.

The Williams' flat was on Prairie Street (later it became Highland Boulevard) between Seventh and Eighth streets, and Pabst Brewery was at the top of the hill. All night long I heard those big old Pabst horses going **PLOC-IT-A, PLOC-IT-A,** and the wagon wheels rumbling by the house. It was Prohibition so I don't know what they were hauling to the railroad tracks down by the Milwaukee River. Anyhow, I didn't get much sleep on my wedding night.

The next morning when I looked out, it was grey, just grey. I'd never seen anything like it. There'd been a snowstorm in April and wagons were hauling sooty chunks of snow to the river. I felt as if I was in a foreign land: Milwaukee was the ugliest, greyest town I'd ever seen!

For the first weeks of marriage I was homesick. Everything was strange—I didn't even know my husband. The first thing I did was write to Bessie, mama and papa. One day a letter came from Bessie that said George Washington Carver had come to Texarkana to speak and stayed with her and James. There was Bessie with a famous man in her house, and here I was, in a strange place with no work. Then a job found me.

IN THE DARK AT THE MAJESTIC

Willard's Aunt Alberta got me a job as an usher at the Majestic Theater where she worked, in the Majestic Building on Grand Avenue; later, officials re-named it "Wisconsin Avenue" to match the name east of the Milwaukee River. The big shows came from New York. Jimmy Durante. Ethel Barrymore. Fred Waring. Sophie Tucker. The Majestic didn't show silent films, but later I read that there were forty-four movie houses in the city by 1912. The theater worked light colored girls as usherettes because Jessie, the head usher, had a German mother and a black father, and she did the hiring.

The first night, I reported to work in my new usherette outfit: a black dress with white collar, cuffs and apron, with a tiny cap pinned to my hair. The management didn't let us have flashlights and we had to remember all the rows from the top on down. That night I was on the wall aisle. In the middle aisles we had to seat people right and left. Starting at the bottom meant the wall aisle.

The music began, the house went dark and people were waiting at the door to be seated. It seemed like they all wanted to sit on my side of the theater, and a crowd came and piled up in the middle of my aisle. Lord, I didn't know where I was! I was feeling around to find the seats and my aisle was clogged with grumbling people.

"Get these people out of here!" a man scolded.

"I'm doin' the best I can!" I said. I didn't know the man was Jim Hilger, the manager, until someone told me.

After I worked there awhile, sometimes I checked coats. Raccoon coats were the rage and they were huge heavy things. One night a man came in a long raccoon coat.

"How can a little thing like you hang this coat?" he said. "I'll bet you can't even lift it!"

"I can manage," I said.

He laughed and handed me the coat, and it was so heavy I almost toppled over with it. But I hung it and he gave me a big tip.

One of the usherettes was Betty, a birch-skinned girl who had a black boyfriend, Abe. The Majestic had two live shows a day—a matinee and an evening show. Betty knew better, but she bought an orchestra row ticket for Abe for the evening performance, and after the lights went out Abe slipped in and took his seat. He was supposed to sit in the balcony—"nigger heaven," some called it. The people sitting around Abe protested to the manager, he made Abe get out, and Betty almost lost her job.

It didn't seem right, because Wisconsin had an anti-discrimination law. In 1889 a railroad porter, Owen Howell, had sued a Milwaukee theater owner because he couldn't sit in the parquet. It was a landmark court decision: Howell won. And a civil rights law against discrimination in restaurants and other public places was proposed by a black Milwaukee attorney, William T. Green, and was passed in 1905 by the Wisconsin legislature. The problem was, no one seemed to know the laws existed and they acted like they always had.

The Majestic didn't pay a lot, but I made quite a bit in tips. I didn't want Willard to feel as if I was supporting him, because jobs were hard to find and he felt bad enough when he was out of work. So I gave him my paycheck and let him handle the money, and late at night we'd sit on the bed and count the tips.

Willard had worked for a big lumber man whose family was English. He lived with his wife, mother and sister and they had high tea and low tea in Milwaukee! The man had got kind of kooky and needed somebody as a companion, because if he went downtown he bought a hundred of this and a hundred of that. He'd had a white boy working for him and he quit, and a social service worker got Willard the job. Willard worked there quite awhile and didn't have to do anything but go around with the man. Then the white boy decided to come back and that threw Willard out of work just before we were married.

Willard had usually worked in hotels and he was ambitious. He had a beautiful tenor voice and sang on the radio sometimes with the Urban League Male Chorus. But he never got a solo, even though everybody said he had the best voice in the group.

"I've had some fine voice teachers," he said, "but the trouble is, I never learned to play an instrument—I always have trouble getting an accompanist."

He was depressed and I knew the real reason was that he wasn't working. I didn't have sense enough to be worried about Willard being out of work because we were living with Octavia and Robert, at 717 Prairie Avenue. West of 27th Street, Prairie was called "Highland."

A rich Greek family lived downstairs and Mr. Hahn, the owner of our duplex, had a big house two doors away. There was another brick house that belonged to his wife.

"People say she has it in her will that she always wants a Negro family to live in the house," Octavia said. I don't know if it was true, but that was the only Negro family living on that side of the street. But they weren't the first ones to live there. Next to them, some Polish people lived and next to them was a natatorium. On the north corner was a popular German place, Liedertafel Hall.

"The Germans have dances and festivals," Willard said.

"And the Hungarians have a Grape Harvest Festival," Octavia added.

They were trying to explain everything in the neighborhood. The German and Russian Jewish cultures in our area were new and colorful to me. Up the street was the Vocational School.

Willard and I walked everywhere. I wanted to see Lake Michigan and we walked downtown, crossed the bridge and walked to the Northwestern Depot at the end of Grand Avenue. Nearby, as we sat on the rocks and let the waves lap at our feet, I didn't imagine that in years to come the shoreline would be pushed out hundreds of feet and that the depot would be destroyed when I was old.

As weeks passed and warm weather came, I liked Milwaukee. It wasn't all greyness and clomping horses. I'd never been in a big city except for visiting Dallas, hadn't been in a movie house or seen streetcars. Adjusting would have been a terrible ordeal if it hadn't been for the people. Milwaukee was like a big country town, the people were so friendly.

People who visited had calling cards and one day some acquaintances of Octavia's came to meet me. All their names started with "B": Dr. and Mrs. Badger—he was a dentist; Dr. and Mrs. Baylor—he was the leading chiropodist in the city; and Dr. and Mrs. Boeger. Dr. Boeger and Dr. Allen Herron were the first Negroes to graduate from Marquette Medical School. Dr. Herron was a noted physician and he lived to be about ninety years old.

"I'm so pleased to meet you," Minnie Badger said. "I'm from Georgia, so I know what an adjustment you must be going through." She was older than I was, but over the following years she became my best friend.

"How did you like your callers?" Octavia asked me after they'd gone.

"Oh, they were nice, especially Minnie Badger," I said.

"I knew you'd like them," Octavia said. Then she chuckled, "What did you think of the Baylors?"

"Dr. Baylor's almost as short as I am—but I liked his goutee!" I said. "Does Mrs. Baylor dye her hair red?"

Octavia laughed until tears rolled down her cheeks.

"You just asked what everybody's been wonderin' for years!" she said, wiping her eyes with her hanky. "Her hair seems too nappy to be natural red, but they come from the East and they do things different out there."

"I liked her jewelry," I said, not wanting to seem ungrateful.

"She wears plenty of it to like!" Octavia chuckled. "Crooks her fingers in them little gloves and puts on airs, but her heart's as gold as them rings an' things. You ever need help, don't sell Mrs. Baylor short!"

The callers weren't Willard's best friends, but they knew him and accepted me right away. Pretty soon, we had a dinner group; we met in our homes about once a month and the women took turns preparing dinner.

DISCRIMINATION

At first, I didn't feel any discrimination in the North because most of Willard's friends were Polish boys. He had so many white friends who came to the house that it was strange to me.

But after I saw how Abe was treated at the Majestic, Willard told me about something that had happened to an old family friend before I moved to Milwaukee. Cora Miller had gone to the Butterfly Theater with a white friend—I think her name was Mrs. Wilson—and Cora got in line in front of her friend. The white people in front of Cora all got tickets and then Cora came to the ticket booth.

"All the tickets are sold!" the woman in the booth said.

So Cora stepped out of line, her white friend stepped up and the woman in the booth sold her a ticket. They had her right there! Cora sued and Willard said that she got a few hundred dollars.

It didn't seem so bad now because Willard and I could go almost every place, I suppose because I was so light. But we knew we weren't supposed to go into nice restaurants and that friends who'd tried to eat in them were treated badly, so we didn't try. The only nice place where minorities felt welcome was at Charley Toy's original restaurant, so that's where we went for special occasions.

And business people wouldn't hire Negroes or anyone with mixed blood. They didn't mind talking to you, and they'd call you "Mister" and "Missus," but they wouldn't give you a job.

"This prejudice thing just got bad after the war," Willard said. "I was color-blind and didn't know there was any difference between people until Booker T. Washington came and gave a speech!"

"No use in my applying to teach," I said. "I'm not certified, and they wouldn't hire me if I was."

"It's a good thing you didn't like teaching all that much," Willard said. "Nothing worse than having your heart set on work no one'll give you a chance to try!"

I'd worked about a year at the theater when movies came to the Majestic and put me out of a job. Then I worked at a hosiery factory until the manager found out I was part black. He was a dwarf and he came and stood back of me and watched me work for a long time. Somebody must have pointed me out to him and that was the only time I ever lied: I said I was Canadian because I needed a job. They began to find fault with my work, everything was wrong, then they fired me. The girl that hired me cried, she was so sorry.

OCTAVIA

Willard's mother gave me so much support, I loved her from the start and called her "Mother." She was pretty, with beautiful dark skin and hair, but she was only five feet tall and so fat! She'd had a hard life because her mother put her out to work when she was fifteen and that's how she met Heard and got married. She wasn't but sixteen years older than Willard.

Robert was about six foot tall, thin, and handsome, with straight hair. He'd been a railroad man and that used to be a big thing, to be a railroad man. Willard and I laughed when they went down the street because Robert stepped long and mother waddled along behind, trying to catch up.

Octavia told me that she divorced her second husband because he was a gambler.

"One day we'd have everything and the next day we didn't have nothin'!" she said. "He made us a good living, but I never knew where we stood. He had a tavern on the corner of 3rd and Wells, next to Johnny Walker's, and could have bought Johnny Walker's for a little of nothing, but he didn't do it. But it was the gamblin' that got me—I couldn't stand that gamblin' part!"

Maybe that's why she always told us to try to save a dollar a day. If we'd listened and done that, we wouldn't have had to go through the tragedy we did later. Mother knew how to provide. She didn't have much education but she always worked, usually as a maid. She worked at the Plankinton and Wisconsin Hotels, and she was friendly to everybody, like Willard.

"How can you be friends with everybody right off the bat?" I asked.

"As easy to be a friend as a foe," Mother said.

Here's an incident that shows how mother treated everyone. The Urban League was small and the Kerns came here and didn't know anybody in Milwaukee. Mr. Kern was head of the Urban League in the 1920s, and when he was at the depot one of the redcaps told him that Mrs. Kinner had a room for boarders. A lot of the boys sent people there and they all still called her "Mrs. Kinner" because she hadn't been married to Robert Williams for long. So Mr. and Mrs. Kern came to Octavia's apartment and they never forgot how she made them feel at home. They always talked about that.

Her mother, Grandma Victoria Black, was lovable, too, and had long white hair down to her waist. She stayed at Aunt Ollie's until later, when she came to live with us.

Mr. Hahn had built our duplex, and his wealth showed in the stained glass window above the stairway, the big front room with a sliding door, and the parlor we used for a living room. Mother and Robert slept in the front room and we slept in the bedroom off the dining room.

Mrs. Kelly's room was above ours and we could hear her drop her shoes at night.

"Mrs. Kelly's going to bed!" we'd laugh when we heard the first shoe drop. We'd wait for the other one to plop, then we could roll over and go to sleep if we were through counting tips. Almost everybody kept roomers because they needed money.

But the Greek family downstairs raised money in other ways. We had an alley along our backyard and one week toward the end of summer, trucks came and they unloaded boxes of grapes and hauled them into our basement. More trucks came and they unloaded fifty-pound sacks of sugar and lugged them to the basement.

"Wine-making time," Willard said.

"Pretty soon the place'll smell like a Speakeasy!" Octavia said. "It always does, every fall."

In a few weeks you could smell that wine all over the neighborhood, and it was Prohibition! People got around it in a lot of ways and wealthy people had more parties than anybody thought of having in the Thirties. They didn't know what was ahead. I know, because our next jobs were for rich East-siders.

A friend and his wife "worked family": he was a chauffeur and she was a cook. He wanted to go to Chicago, so they asked us to take their job and Willard was eager, but I held back.

"I don't know anything about that!" I said. "I can't even cook, except for cakes!"

"Here I thought you were being polite, staying out of mother's way in the kitchen," Willard teased.

"I can't help it if I had mama to do the cookin'!" I said. "Papa never would let me work in any white kitchen." Maybe memories of what mama'd told me about white kitchens were making me afraid.

"Honey, we need work," he said. "There's nothing to be afraid of—I've worked for families all of my life, and I'll help you."

So we took the job to work for the John Apple s* on the East side and I was wondering if I'd be able to learn to cook, or if we'd get fired when they found out I didn't know what I was doing.

7

"Working Family"

The first angelfood cake I made was in the Apples'* kitchen. We didn't know how important the name "angelfood" would be to us in three years, and we didn't know it would mean disaster by the end of the Depression.

Mrs. Apple was one of these women who didn't want to do anything! I had to plan the meals, do the buying and learn to cook out of a Boston School (Fanny Farmer) cookbook. The first time I made a schaumtorte it was flat and hard, and I was in a tizzy! "That's all right, that's all right!" Mrs. Apple said. I was discovering that she was a lovely woman with nice friends, like Mrs. Heil, Governor Heil's wife. During our first months there, I almost slept with that cookbook! I don't know how many disasters I served because nobody said anything. Not even Sammy.*

Sammy was the Apples' adopted boy who'd been found wrapped in newspaper in an alley. He was handsome, but had a withered arm and a mental problem. "When my mama and daddy's gone," he'd say, "I'm the boss of this house!" Nobody paid attention to his remarks and he followed Willard and me everywhere.

He had everything in the world any child could want because the Apples were older and Mrs. Apple lavished everything on him, but Sammy'd steal. They sent him to the University School where rich people sent their kids, and he'd steal gloves and bikes. He'd take a bike, ride it a piece, throw it in a ditch and the school would call. It broke his mother's heart that he was in hot water all the time, with people calling, "Sammy did this, Sammy did that!" But I don't think Mrs. Apple ever regretted adopting him, she loved him

60

so much. It got so I didn't tell her about all the complaints, I felt so sorry for her.

UP IN THE AIR OVER BILLY MITCHELL'S SISTER

The Apple s dressed formally to go to parties in Milwaukee's high society and one day Mrs. Apple was talking to her husband about a big occasion.

"George, I need a new dress," she said.

"Another one?" Mr. Apple said. "What's wrong with the one you wore to the Heils' party?"

"General Billy Mitchell's sister is going to be there," she said. "She never wears the same gown twice. I think I'll have a gown custom-made."

"There's nothing like a custom-customer," Mr. Apple muttered, and it was the end of the discussion.

A few weeks later on the evening of the big affair, Mrs. Apple came downstairs lookin' shiny as a Lake Michigan alewife in a floor-length black gown, all shimmery with silver beads. Even her husband was impressed, and Mrs. Apple was beaming when they left for the party.

Willard went to bed early and I'd put Sammy to bed, but it wasn't late when I heard Apple s pull into the drive. A car door slammed, then I heard the car pulling into the garage, so I went to open the door for Mrs. Apple, and her expression told me she was in a stew.

"I didn't know it was so late," I said, taking her cape.

"It isn't late!" she said and stomped upstairs.

"I'll be right up to turn down your bed!" I called after her. I hung the cape in the closet and went to open the back door for Mr. Apple. All the while I was wondering why Mrs. Apple had her dander up. "I didn't know it was so late," I said to Mr. Apple.

"It isn't late—thank you, Reg." He handed me his hat and looked at his pocket watch. "It's only nine-thirty."

He walked quietly through the kitchen, into the living room and picked up a book by his chair, then sat and opened it as if he was going to read. I knew better. Wasn't going to be any reading done that night! I put his hat on the closet shelf and hurried upstairs.

"G'night, Mr. Apple!" I called.

"Good-night, Regie," he said quietly.

I was passing the Apple's room when she called to me.

"Come in here, Regie," she said. The door was open and I stepped in. Mrs. Apple was in her robe with the beaded dress draped over her arm. I was about to ask what she wanted me for, when she pushed the dress into my arms. "You can have it!" she said.

"Wh—why on earth?" I stuttered.

"It's yours," she said. Her lips were pursed and she turned to brush her hair. I knew I was dismissed, so I picked up the dress and hurried to the door.

"Thank you, Mrs. Apple," I said, then hurried down the hall to our room.

I couldn't tell Willard the news because he was sleeping. I thought I might wake him if I pulled the chain for the ceiling bulb, so I laid the dress over a chair and lit the kerosene lamp. As I lifted the dress, the black beads flickered with the flame of the lamp, and I thought I'd never seen anything so beautiful—at least, not in my closet! It was days before Mrs. Apple told me why she gave me the dress.

"You remember how I said General Billy Mitchell's sister never wore the same dress twice, don't you, Reg?" she said. She'd come into the kitchen to talk while I was doing dishes, and was sitting at the table drinking coffee.

"Mm-hmm. I remember," I said.

"Well, she was already at the party when we arrived and was surrounded by people, but I could see her face and hairdo—she looked stunning. When George and I finally got to her, I saw she was wearing a brown gown with amber beads." Mrs. Apple sat her cup down hard. "Except for the color, her dress was exactly like mine! Everybody saw it right away."

"What a shame!" I said, coming to sit across from her.

"We greeted each other and tried to pretend we didn't notice that we were almost twins, then I told George I wanted to leave. I couldn't enjoy myself, especially after he made a remark about my $150 'custom' dress. Honestly, sometimes it seems like all he thinks about is money!"

I didn't say anything, because I could see Mr. Apple's side of the picture. Besides, I didn't want to say anything that might make Mrs. Apple change her mind and ask for the dress back!

Mr. Apple wasn't the only one with money on his mind; Sammy began to steal from us. He'd go in our room and take money, but I never told his mother about it. Once, we had quarters on a table and I knew Sammy took them. For his sake more than ours, I was trying to teach him right.

"Sammy, give me those quarters!" I said. He reached down in his shirt and pulled out twenty-five dollars in paper money that he'd taken and we didn't know he had!

But Sammy didn't get much of our money, and we saved and bought our first car, a used 1919 Ford with curtains. We named it "Sparkplug," after the comicstrip.

Then the Apples got into hard luck and had to cut down on everything, so Mrs. Apple got Mrs. Schultz* to take us. But Mrs. Apple and I became lifelong friends and corresponded for years after they moved to California much later. Before they left, one day Mrs. Apple laughed, "I knew you didn't know how to cook when you came!"

Poor Sammy, he died at twenty-five. I reckon it was a good thing because he was a born thief.

WORKING FOR SCHULTZ'S

Frederick and Helen Schultz, their children and her mother lived on Milwaukee's East side among stately brick homes near Lake Michigan. Mr. Schultz had an automobile franchise.

They'd only had Germans work in their home and later, Mrs. Schultz told me that she was scared and didn't know how I might be. Willard worked as the butler-houseman and I was the cook. I made the beds for him and he did the scrubbing for me, so I never had to scrub. Mrs. Schultz had a German laundry lady and she wondered how we were going to get along. We became close friends; she was so fond of me, she'd do my laundry.

Mrs. Schultz and I were almost like sisters, we were so close. They had an eleven-year-old son, Henry,* and a five or six-year-old daughter, Caroline.* The Schultz's weren't much older than we were and went a lot, so I almost raised the kids. I'd have to get them off to school and their mother taught them to mind us. They were wonderful children! Mrs. Schultz trusted me so much, she'd planned this trip to go to New York with Mrs. Randall—they were the Bradford piano people—and everything was arranged. Caroline had her appendix out shortly before, was home recuperating and Mrs. Schultz went to New York and left her with me because she knew I'd take care of her.

The master bedroom was downstairs, and the children had rooms on second floor, around the corner from ours. Across the hall was grandma's room; Mrs. Schultz's mother, Mrs. Fry,* lived with them.

I found that among rich white families, most old people talked about their children, no matter how good they were to them. Mrs. Fry was an English widow who'd been wealthy and she turned up her nose at Mr. Schultz because he was German. And he was supporting her, letting her live in their house! Grandma'd had both breasts removed for cancer and was in her eighties. She wanted to go every place with Helen, so when Helen went without her, grandma'd get on the phone and call Helen's friends and talk about her.

"Oh, Grandma, what are you doin' that for?" I'd ask. She loved me and I called her "Grandma" like the kids.

Mr. Schultz never had anything to do with us and anything he wanted done, Helen told us. Every first of the month he gave her allowances—so much for clothes, so much for food. So much for grandma. They gave her a good living but when they had company they didn't have her down for dinner; she'd eat with the children in the breakfast room off the kitchen. I don't know what happened between Mr. Schultz and grandma, but one time he got so mad, he came into the kitchen and talked to us for the first time, about all the things he'd paid for. It had cost him a lot of money for the operation to have grandma's breasts cut off, but behind his back she called him "a German!"

There was an open staircase in the front hall and when Mr. and Mrs. Schultz had company, grandma'd get the kids to hang over the rail and try to see what was going on. And Mr. Schultz got so mad!

We entertained, too, but grandma wasn't hanging over the railing because we'd wait until she'd gone to the lake with the

64

family. Mrs. Schultz let us entertain our friends in her living room every Saturday night when they'd gone to their home at Pine Lake; she knew all my friends by name.

"Call Minnie Badger," or "Call Mrs. Boeger," she'd say, and even buy food for them. We'd have a big party right in her living room and I don't know what the neighbors thought! "The only thing I want you to do is clean up and not leave the living room a mess," she said. "I don't want Mr. Schultz to know!"

Because of Prohibition, every fall they had a wine man come by and make wine, so they had barrels of wine in the basement. Rich people had all the liquor they wanted—gin and everything else. Willard carried a key to the wine cellar but Frederick wasn't supposed to know. At one party we must have been having such a big time that Willard left wine dripping from a barrel, and the next day Mrs. Schultz came to me.

"Mr. Schultz found a barrel dripping," she said.

But he never said anything to us. Maybe he appreciated that I tried to take good care of him. He wanted to sleep when they'd been out late, and they went out almost every night. (We did the same thing—we'd have our car and wonder who was going to get home first!) The next morning if the phone rang I'd answer.

"Is Mr. Schultz there?" somebody'd ask.

"Oh, no," I'd say. "He just left."

"That's all right, Reg!" sometimes a man would laugh. "This is Mr. Randall. Let him sleep!"

Dr. Hart* across the street was on the staff at Columbia Hospital. The Hart's were older, but Schultz's went back and forth with them. Schultz's belonged to The Deutscher Club (it became The Wisconsin Club) and they'd take the Harts and other friends there to eat. One night I was preparing a dinner for them, they were playing high society and Mr. Schultz didn't know whether to put on his tuxedo or wear his street-clothes. He was in a suit and he looked across the street and here came Dr. Hart out his front door in a tuxedo, so Mr. Schultz ran upstairs to get into his tuxedo fast!

"Reg, let's have a spring lamb for Christmas," Mrs. Schultz said one year.

"Lamb in December's gonna shoot the budget," I said.

"I want something different," she said.

So we ordered the different meal. Then we got the different bill: eighteen dollars!

"Now we have to economize or Frederick will have a fit!" Mrs. Schultz said.

We had a big laugh about that. She'd go to her clubs and afterwards she'd come in the kitchen and tell me everything that happened. Oh, I loved that woman! She was so close to me, I think I was her best friend.

But after awhile, Willard and I had a problem when grandma began coming into our room at any time of night—she'd walk in without knocking. I didn't mind, but Willard didn't like it. He told Mr. or Mrs. Schultz, and I sure did hate it when he told them. Mrs. Schultz wanted to send grandma to a nursing home right away and it hurt grandma awful bad.

"Please let me stay," she cried. "Oh, don't send me to that place!"

I felt awful about it, but The Lutheran Home for the Aged was beautiful, on a hill on Twenty-Second Street between Wells and State. It cost a lot to keep her there, but she was unhappy; I don't think grandma would have been happy anywhere. Mrs. Schultz wanted Willard and me to look after her, and we went to see her every Sunday in their car. Sometimes I didn't want to, but we'd take grandma to the cemetery or a show, and they'd take her to Pine Lake, but grandma was unhappy at the Home.

PINE LAKE

George Mader was a young guy who worked for Mr. Schultz and sometimes he'd chauffeur the kids and me to the movies. Later, he started a little German restaurant called "Mader's."

But Willard and I drove our own car when we all went to Pine Lake after school was out. One year we got up early and left long before Schultz's. We were chugging along in Sparkplug when Schultz's come along and passed us in the big car and got to the lake long ahead of us.

"Frederick, you've got to get Reg and Willard a car!" Mrs. Schultz said. So Mr. Schultz got us a little Phaeton with two seats and a rumbleseat and we named it "Rudy."

I couldn't see my friends out at the lake and I hated it as much as Mrs. Schultz, but Willard and I had our own cottage with running water and electric lights. Most all the rich Germans had summer homes there, including a Mr. Beggs who was a millionaire from St. Louis. He had an island that they called "Beggs' Island," and he owned the transit company in Milwaukee.

It wasn't compulsory for us to go with the children, but Mrs. Schultz liked me to take care of them. Henry and Caroline had friends who lived across the lake—most everybody had launches. The Schultz's had a rowboat and the kids loved the water, but Willard and I couldn't swim. One night the children wanted to go across the lake in the rowboat to visit their friends. Henry begged and begged, Willard was ready to go because he'd do anything, and I finally consented to get in the rowboat with only a small flashlight and no lifejackets. We rowed out and halfway across the lake, here came a launch! The waves began to rock, **wwww, wwww, wwww!** Henry had sense enough to hold up the light so the people in the launch saw us and stopped. I was never so afraid in my life!

The nearest picture show was at Oconomowoc but we never could go by ourselves. "Can't you get Reg to go to the show tonight?" Mrs. Schultz would ask Willard.

"I'll see what I can do," he'd say.

Then he'd tell me we were taking her and the children again. Mr. Schultz wouldn't let her go to Oconomowoc unless we were with her. She couldn't force us because after supper our time was our own, so she'd never ask me, she'd ask Willard.

One night we took Mrs. Schultz and the children to Oconomowoc, and it was always awful because Willard and I were the only colored ones in the theater. "The Shiek of Araby" was playing and, as we walked in, a blacked man came out on the stage and said, "I'm the Shiek of Alabam!" Everyone turned and looked at us and Mrs. Schultz didn't like it, but we didn't think it was aimed at us. It was supposed to be a little comedy.

My family was far away, but our ties stayed strong. Bessie came to visit and stayed at Octavia's while she was here.

After she left, we wrote as much as ever, and papa and I wrote every month. Minnie was busy with her children and we kind of drifted apart, but once in awhile I'd send clothes for her kids, and one year she wrote and asked if she could name their new son "Willard Kenneth," after Willard. Of course, he said "Yes!"

We'd been saving the money we earned at Schultz's and, finally, in 1924, we decided it was time to spend some of it on a trip: we were going home to Washington!

8
From Jim Crow, to a Teashop

Willard was scared to death to go South. He hadn't been there since he was seven, and he'd been reading about lynchings and Jim Crow Cars. Friends from St. Louis had visited and told us what they did on trains.

"We get in the Jim Crow Car to start with," they said, "then we don't have the humiliation of having to move from the regular car."

Poplar Bluff, Missouri, was the dividing line where a conductor came into a passenger car and said, "Get out! Get out!" and made Negroes move into a Jim Crow Car. That included anyone with a drop of African blood in his veins. We talked it over and decided to do as our friends said. It was our first long trip together and we planned for weeks. Papa and Bessie wrote about how excited they and mama were, and my head was filled with thoughts of them and Washington.

The day we left, we were staying at Octavia's because we were on our two-week vacation from Schultz's, so she and Robert waved to us from the porch as we lugged our bags onto the Seventh Street streetcar at the corner. A few blocks south, we transferred to the Grand Avenue line and soon we were at the Milwaukee Depot. Willard looked smart in his suit and tie when he stepped up to the ticket window. We were early, but after about half an hour the train pulled in, we boarded, and the conductor examined our tickets and gestured toward the parlor car. From Chicago to St. Louis, we were putting on the dog!

"I never thought I'd ride in a parlor car!" I said as we sank onto the plush seats in the big compartment.

"We have to go in style while we can!" Willard grinned.

We had to laugh because we knew that after St. Louis we'd be creepin' home in any car they'd let us sit in. My heart pounded with happiness as the train picked up speed. Clicks of the wheels came closer together and the car began to sway as the countryside flew by the window. We were on our way home!

In St. Louis we changed trains and climbed into the Jim Crow Car—it was like any other cheap train. Not worse, nothing fancy. I didn't think anything of it because I'd been riding Jim Crow Cars all my life, but I noticed that Willard was quiet.

Arkansas was a dry state (the whole country was supposed to be!) but we were taking a bottle of wine to mama and papa. Willard bought it from the Greeks downstairs from his mother's place and we had it in a suitcase. We were half-talking and half-watching the scenery, when we heard someone say that investigators were searching luggage. Then two men came into our car. Willard got so scared when he saw them coming, he opened the suitcase and grabbed the bag with the bottle in it. He jumped up and fumbled at the window slides, but just as he was going to throw the wine out, the men walked by. Willard sat down, still shaking. But the wine went back in the baggage!

Bessie was as bubbly as champagne when she met us at the Hope train station. "It sure is good to have you home!" she laughed, and we hugged and chattered as she led us to her Model T. "Mama's so excited, she's been cooking for two weeks!"

"I hope she has sweet potatoes and cornbread," I said, mouth watering at the thought of mama's cooking. But my throat was tight and stomach churning as we bumped past the cotton fields, toward Washington. At last we came to a woods, passed some houses with big yards, and we were home.

Jennie'd already run out to greet us by the time mama and papa came out on the porch. My sister had always been straight as a stick, and now she was as round as a Tom Watson watermelon, she'd gained so much weight.

"Is this your mother?" Willard asked.

"No, I'm Jennie!" she said.

70

Poor Willard! But everyone laughed, and soon he and papa were sitting on the porch, visiting like old friends. All my family took to him right off. Papa was crazy about him, he really loved him, and over the years Willard was good to him. Willard was like papa wanted a son to be, and papa was the father that Willard had always wanted.

Washington had changed: the houses had electric lights, thanks to Mr. Stout and Mr. Betton. And there were a lot of new people, including a white family who'd bought a store about a block from home.

Willard was so scared of the South, he didn't even want to get razor blades at the store, so I told him to go by himself to get used to things. When he came back, he chuckled and told us about a pretty white salesgirl who had waited on him. He asked for the blades, she got them and when he asked how much they were, she drawled, "Own—ly fif—ty ci—aynts!" Willard got such a kick out of her accent, he told that story for years.

We stayed in Arkansas for two weeks and, looking back, I think we should have spent more time with my parents, bu we went to visit Bessie in Texarkana. She and James were or the verge of divorce and he wasn't home, so I never saw James after my marriage, and he and I had been close. One day, Bessie was driving us around Texarkana and pointed to a grove of trees.

"It was about there where they lynched that black man," she said. I'd heard about the lynching because it happened before I moved to Milwaukee, so she told it for Willard's benefit. "A white woman owned a Pierce Arrow, and a black man bought one, too—I don't recall who owned one first. Anyhow, some white men told him that he couldn't drive the same model as this rich lady. They said he'd have to get rid of his car. Well, the man wanted to keep his car—"

"I can't blame him for that!" Willard said.

"I can't either," Bessie said, "but they lynched him for it. Hung him right about there." Bessie had driven around the block and stopped in front of the grove of trees. Willard looked at the spot hard and long before we drove on.

Our vacation went by too fast for me, but Willard was happy when we headed North again, even on the Jim Crow Car!

* * *

We went back to "working family" for Schultz's in Milwaukee, and a few months later our lives were changed by a new hotel.

The Shorecrest Hotel on Prospect Avenue was new and popular, some of Mrs. Schultz's friends had moved there, and she wanted to move there. So Schultz's sold their house and got ready to move into an apartment at the hotel, and we wondered what we'd do next. We talked about my dream of owning a teashop, but we couldn't afford it. There was another complication: they might have liked puttin' on the dog, but Schultz's had one dog too many.

Their fox terrier, Jill, had papers and they'd bred her and she'd had five puppies. Pal was the only male, so Schultz's had sold the other puppies and kept him. But they couldn't keep the male and female together, and they wouldn't have room to separate them at the Shorecrest. Mrs. Schultz knew I was crazy about Pal. She also wanted to keep Jill. But Mr. Schultz wanted to keep Pal and get rid of Jill. Guess who won?!

"Regie, I know you love Pal so much," Mrs. Schultz said, "I'm going to give him to you!"

Mr. Schultz being a gentleman, he didn't say anything.

Pal was solid white except for a small brown spot, and he looked like the champion terrier worth $10,000. Everybody was crazy about that dog! So we moved back to Octavia's with a new family member.

Then we began to look for work. Willard was hired at The Surf again and I found a job as an elevator operator at the Milwaukee Library. Someone said that books about home brewing were having the biggest circulation, and I thought it was a joke until I read it in a history book. When I took the job I didn't know that a librarian named Goldie Mabowetz had left there in 1921—the year that I came to Milwaukee. Goldie and many Jewish immigrants had lived on Walnut Street, a few blocks from Willard. She and her husband, Morris Myerson, had taken a train from the same depot where Hollis Kinner had met us on our wedding night. Then they took a long boat trip to Palestine. The librarian was Golda Meir.

At first, I thought that the top floor of the library was as high as I was going that year, but soon I was filling out an application for a job as a cook at The Surf restaurant, where Willard and Mrs. Kelly worked. She was moving to a home she had in Michigan and the restaurant needed another cook, so that's how I came to The Surf.

THE SURF RESTAURANT

The Surf was in the old Baldwin home in the 1500 block of Prospect Avenue on a bluff overlooking the lake. It was a mansion with huge halls, wide staircases and big dining rooms. The manager, Mrs. Nicholson, had a few apartments upstairs, but mainly she ran The Surf. Everything was by reservation. And did she get reservations, she gave so much food for the price!

Willard had worked at The Surf so much through the years, that some people thought he owned it! He wore a tuxedo and almost ran it. Then he served liquor at private parties at the restaurant and the Bartenders' Union got after Mrs. Nicholson, so he had to get a bartender's license. We had keys to the front door of the restaurant because I cooked breakfast and had to be the first one there. Mrs. Nicholson trusted us completely.

"Regie, you bring me good luck!" Mrs. Nicholson said.

She had red hair down to her waist and said, "I'm shanty Irish!" in a thick brogue. With fair skin and freckles on her nose, she was Irish to the bone. Oh, I loved her!

Another Irish lady named Rose was a cook. Mrs. Nicholson'd stand at the head of the basement stairs and Rose'd be at the foot and they'd be yelling at each other in thick Irish while we were laughing in the kitchen. Those two Irish ladies did work, and I never could understand why any business would have put a **"NO IRISH NEED APPLY"** sign on a door.

Some people said Mrs. Nicholson was a widow, but I think she was divorced because she couldn't marry in the Catholic Church. Anyhow, she had a gentleman friend and they couldn't get married. But the bishop of the Milwaukee Archdiocese often came to The Surf and once a year she'd have a big whitefish dinner with his favorite food and champagne. When the chef wasn't there, I'd help broil and baste the fish.

The chef drank a lot and anytime he fell out, I'd have to fall in! Once we had some big parties going, the chef didn't show up and there I was, running around trying to cook and make up over a hundred servings!

73

"People at the last tables in that party of a hundred's getting antsy!" said the waitress.

"Reckon they'll have to be antsy!" I grumbled. "I'm goin' as fast as I can!" I was tossing ham and poking potatoes and vegetables on plates, and it bothered me that I couldn't take the time to make each one look like a picture. Besides the big party, we had groups of thirty-five and sixteen. No time to play with parsley that night!

Mr. Clarenbach, the accountant, would get mad at Mrs. Nicholson because she didn't count the price, she just wanted beautiful dinners and was always up to her neck in debt.

"You've got to stop adding trimmings and centerpieces," he said. "If you stick to the menu, the cost of a dinner will be about $1.35 and you can make fifteen or twenty cents a plate."

"Begorra, if you say so, I'll try," she said. She'd stay with the accountant's plan for about a week, then begin adding frills and soon she'd be serving everything again, like big handmade baskets filled with ice cream and beautiful stuff because she cared more about pleasing her customers than about profit.

Meanwhile, customers got to know Willard and me, and we began getting calls to cater private parties for wealthy families. I loved making fancy things like baked Alaska, and I liked trimming food to look fine. I was gaining experience that would soon be put to good use.

THE OLD LUTZ MANSION, DREAM COME TRUE

"Wouldn't it be nice to have a place of our own?" I'd say to Willard when we were counting tips on the bed. Magazine pictures of teashops still floated in my mind.

"It'd be nice but we can't afford it yet."

"Milwaukee could use a nice restaurant for Negroes."

"Maybe next year."

We missed hearing Mrs. Kelly's shoes clunk since she'd moved, but Octavia had other boarders, usually Marquette students. One was a graduate of Marquette Medical School who brought his sister here to go to the university. But she couldn't get in because they wouldn't admit Negro girls, so she went to the State Teachers' College. Mrs. Zimmerman, a white woman, helped some of the Negro women's organizations and formed a board: Mrs. Delrude, Ida Holly and Minnie Badger were on it. They and Mrs. Zimmerman met with Marquette officials and sat up most of one night arguing. In the end, the university representatives said they didn't have to take anybody they didn't want to because they were a private school.

So segregation was here, even though we weren't always aware of it. And blacks still couldn't eat in nice restaurants. We kept talking about our teashop. I was a dreamer and Willard was a planner. We never had violent quarrels. If one of us was upset, the other would be quiet and we worked it out.

I was taking a correspondence course in hotel and teashop management through Lewis Teashop in Washington, D.C., preparing for the day when we could go into business. At the end of 1925, we went to a real estate dealer, Mr. Pleasant.

"Can you find a house big enough for us to live in, and have a sizeable restaurant, too?" Willard asked.

"Should be able to find something with all these old mansions going up for sale," Mr. Pleasant said. "I'll scout around." A few days later, he stopped by. "I think I've found your house," he said. "A couple of elderly sisters want to sell their family home. You ever heard of Dr. Lutz?"

"Sure," Willard said. "They're a well-known family."

"These old sisters were his daughters," Mr. Pleasant said. "The house is brick, elegant—and it's in good shape."

"Sounds like what we're looking for," Willard said. "Isn't it over on Galena?"

"That's right—615," Mr. Pleasant said. "Neighborhood's past its prime, but there are three old mansions on the block, and it's a central location." Willard and I looked at each other.

"Can we see it tomorrow?" he asked quickly.

The next day, we went to see the house. It was stately, surrounded by lilacs and elms.

The teashop!

We'd found it! After we saw the fireplaces, open staircase and huge rooms, we went home and talked to mother. Octavia was as excited as we were because we could have an upstairs apartment and some rooms for travelers. So with her help, we made a small down payment on our dream. Who'd have believed that in a few years it would turn into a nightmare?

The owner of the real estate company bought the Lutz house for $8,000, then turned around and sold it to us for $12,000 and the sisters were angry when they found out. Even though we paid more than we should have, we were excited: for the first time in our lives, we were going to be our own bosses!

Somehow, a newspaper heard about our plans and on April 17, 1926, two months before we opened, the WISCONSIN ENTERPRISE BLADE ran a two-column story. The headline of the state's first minority newspaper read:

Milwaukee To Have A $25,000.00
Tea Room and Hotel At
615 Galena Street

I didn't see that story or others that editor Anthony Josey wrote about our place until almost sixty years later and I was surprised he played us up so. He wrote:

> The beautiful and costly home of Dr. Lutz, 615 Galena Street, has been purchased by Mr. and Mrs. Willard Heard, through the realty company of Mr. Leon C. Pleasant, and will be remodeled for a first class tea room and hotel, consisting of 12 parlors and dining rooms. This undertaking will fill a long felt need in Milwaukee among our racial group.
>
> Mr. and Mrs. Heard are prominent members of our race and are well prepared to give Milwaukee and the traveling public all that belongs to an up-to-date tea room. In the art of culinary, they are known to prepare food that would tickle the palate of the most fastidious epicurean.
>
> ...The renovation and remodeling, as planned, will be second to none in the northwest. It will be combined with exquisite taste and beauty, portraying technique, French style.
>
> The public should be delighted to welcome and support this new adventure which places Milwaukee in line with other cities. Mr. and Mrs. Heard will do all in their power, sparing neither pains or money, in making their place an ideal resort of comfort and pleasure for the citizens of Milwaukee...

We'd come a long way from the Jim Crow Car!

9

The Angel Food Teashop

The easiest part of going into business was choosing the restaurant's name.

"You're famous for your angelfood cake," Willard said. "Why not call it 'The Angel Food Teashop'?"

So we did. Then we decided to combine our names for the hotel title and had two signs made. The long sign across the top of the porch said WILLAREGE HOTEL, and the one in the yard said ANGEL FOOD TEASHOP.

We had electricity installed in the house, and an intercom system for autophonic music for the upstairs banquet rooms. I was sitting on top of the world, buying crystal at Watts and hundreds of dollars' worth of china and linens at Gimbels.

"If we take in fifty dollars a day, we'll be okay!" I said, but I soon found out different!

The Lutz house was already decorated in good taste, with beige floral wallpaper and carpeted floors. For the windows, I made sheer curtains gathered onto rods at the top and bottom. The three first-floor dining rooms opened to each other; the former dining room would be for private dinner parties. It had sliding doors and an oak table with twelve oak and leather chairs. Mr. and Mrs. Schultz had sold the set to us for almost nothing when they closed up the house and I think they'd paid about $1,000 for it in the early 1900's.

We were caught up in decorating and remodeling when Robert got stabbed. That spring of 1926, Octavia and Robert were like children, almost as excited as we were about the teashop. Then one day Robert was walking home on Seventh Street, between Juneau and Poplar, and a crazy guy came out of the alley and stabbed him. The police caught him later, and Robert didn't even know him. Robert was taken to old Trinity Hospital in critical condition and we visited him as much as we could. Octavia went to the hospital everyday.

"I'm gonna get over to see how that teashop's comin'!" he'd say, but his lungs got worse and he was moved west of the city to Muirdale Tuberculosis Sanitarium.

We were ready to move into our apartment above the teashop (there were six bedrooms upstairs) and Mother Octavia couldn't make up her mind whether to come with us or stay put. She didn't want to break up housekeeping, but with Robert at Muirdale she'd be alone except for boarders. So she wasn't packed on May 26 when our movers came. Then she decided to move with us! The movers had to pack her things and it cost about three hundred dollars. So the first days in our place were bittersweet.

"Somethin's dreadful wrong. Robert just ain't healin'," mother said. He was still at Muirdale on June 12, 1926, on the day of our opening.

Willard was in a tuxedo to greet customers, I was running the kitchen, Pal was barking and bounding up and down the stairs, and the autophonogram was playing Twenties music. The Enterprise-Blade carried a front page article about the opening and listed our first menu. The entrees were fried spring chicken or Virginia baked ham. Other courses and choices included fresh fruit cocktail, spiced pears, cream of mushroom soup, parsley potatoes, buttered green beans, poinsettia salad, strawberry parfait, chocolate nut cake, carmel sundae and, of course, angelfood cake. The price? One dollar. We had specials all week.

Willard always wore his tux and ran the front of the house. I was in charge of the kitchen—the back of the house. I planned the meals, did all the ordering and made the angelfood cakes. We could seat about fifty and a lot of Negroes came that week, but most of them just had a soda and looked around. It took awhile for people to discover us and we had a hard time that summer.

But we had nice friends who placed ads for us, and business began to pick up. People liked the idea of a seven-course dinner in a nice atmosphere for $1.50.

We were surprised that many customers were white.

"Who's your decorator?" they asked. They were astonished to find good taste in an old neighborhood.

"I'm my own decorator!" I laughed.

"Everything tastes so good! What's your secret?"

"Fresh food," I said. "We buy everything fresh."

The kitchen had a hotel-size icebox for meats, chickens, fruits and vegetables. A wholesale place on the South side delivered chickens, and Hassmann-Mueller Foods, across from Usingers on Third Street, brought meat.

Bessie came to visit the month we opened and the Enterprise-Blade carried a front page story:

MISS BESSIE R. DOUGLAS, ARKANSAS, SUPERVISOR NEGRO SCHOOLS, LITTLE RIVER COUNTY

Visiting her sister and brother (in-law), Mr. and Mrs. Willard R. Heard, 615 Galena, is Miss Bessie R. Douglas, Texarkana, Arkansas...Miss Douglas is a member of the A. M. E. church...and was awarded the Jeannes Scholarship to attend Hampton Institute this summer. She is pleasing, entertaining, accomplished, polished and refined.

The social attending she is receiving from Milwaukee will long be remembered. Miss Douglas will remain in Milwaukee until July 6th.

Bessie left shortly before Robert died from the stab wounds to his lungs. He never got to see the teashop. Poor Mother Octavia grieved something awful, but she kept her cleaning job at the hotel and helped us as much as she could. On payday she'd come in with a big package of meat from Yanne Meat Market on State Street.

One day our next door neighbor, Mrs. Charles Uihlein, came for dinner with one of the Lutz sisters and friends. Mrs. Uihlein was the widow of the owner of Uihlein Electric and was as nice as could be. Those ladies couldn't get over how different the house looked with electricity.

The Schroeder Hotel opened about then and a lot of their customers were our customers, too, because word was getting around about our restaurant, and wealthy white people were coming to the teashop. It was surprising how nice some of our competitors were. The manager of the Schroeder came for dinner once a week on his day off and told me what the hotels were doing and serving, to give me ideas. I was becoming well-known for my angelfood cakes and I liked to do fancy cooking, but as soon as I'd made a fancy dish or a dessert like baked Alaska I wanted to try something new. Maybe the variety was the secret of our success.

Or maybe it was the good food and Willard's class. He had a kind of flair and was more extravagant than I was about some things. Many fine restaurants served cigars and cigarettes after dinner, and Willard bought a beautiful cigarette case and every kind of cigarette imaginable. After dinner, he passed them, free, to customers.

Thanks to word-of-mouth reports and a free column, "Willarege Hotel Happenings," that the Enterprise-Blade carried, a regular trade found our teashop. In July we served a five-course dinner for thirty Shorecrest waiters, with Marice Lambert as guest of honor. "The color schemes were beautifully and artistically arranged," according to the paper. "Mr. and Mrs. Heard never tire of exerting their efforts in trying to make things appetizing for their guests..."

The same week, a women's 500 Club met at the teashop, and Mrs. Myrtle Minnieweather accepted position as head waitress. At the end of the month, the Rupert Robinson s of Rockford, Illinois, were guests of the Alfred Taylor s, who entertained them along with Mrs. C. M. Josey and Mr. and Mrs. Edward Jackson, "at the beautiful Willarege Hotel."

By August, the newspaper reported that several "fashionable parties were served at the Willarege Hotel during the past week. The management is very much encouraged by the happy response of Milwaukeeans. Every Wednesday and Saturday is social evening, consisting of music, dancing and games, to which the public is cordially invited."

And the public came. Vivian Graves of Winnetka, Illinois. Dr. H. H. Worlds from Washington, D.C. Elizabeth King of Tampa, Florida. Willard Kennieth of St. Louis, Missouri. Frank Smith from Ogden, Utah. Betty Jones, Mrs. Charles Griggs and the W. W. Kings of Chicago. People named Harris, Harold, Gary and Smith from Racine. Hill and Parks from Madison. Starks, Josey, Baylor, Badger, Claxton and Jefferson from Milwaukee.

Eventually we had a staff of sixteen, including all minority waiters and waitresses. Some of the girls went to State Teachers College, and Eastsiders tried to hire them as maids.

We hadn't been open long before the city changed our street number to 621 W. Galena. Seems like cities like to switch numbers around! No matter what the address was, people were finding the teashop. Our customers came in all varieties, from Marquette students to well-known public figures. Uihleins. Trostels. Judge Shaughnessy. Coach Jennings from Marquette. The board of the State Teachers College. Newsmen from the Milwaukee Journal, the Sentinel and the Wisconsin News. And Mayor Hoan.

Mayor Hoan came often, mainly with political people.

Mrs. Kander, author of The Settlement Cookbook, came. "You've done a good job—I like your teashop," she said. "You did a good job—I use your cookbook!" I laughed.

Mrs. Heil, the future governor's wife, often came with her club.

Once a week the Schultz's neighbor came for ham. He was an English surgeon at Mount Sinai Hospital and was married to a Jewish woman.

A lady from Chicago brought her club every week. She always ordered sweetbreads wrapped in bacon, stuffed mushrooms with peas, and dessert.

Attorney Dereef was older, but he was part of our group, and he often came with friends. Dereef was the first big Negro attorney in Milwaukee after Mr. Green died. His wife taught at Howard University in Washington, but she came to Milwaukee in summer.

But it wasn't all glamor. At first we rented some rooms upstairs to friends and relatives who came from out of town, as the Willarege Hotel. But once in awhile some men would want to rent rooms like in a red light district. We didn't have that kind of place, so Willard would usher them out. The upstairs was mainly for our day-to-day living—we even had Willard's grandma living with us.

Grandma Victoria Black had her own bedroom like mother did. She was in her eighties and had long white hair down to her waist. All the cooks we had there, and grandma insisted on cooking her own food! She'd come down to the kitchen to cook every morning, until she began to get a little fuzzy. Then sometimes she'd come down in the afternoon and think it was morning.

Once some rowdies came in and were getting out of hand, so Willard took a toy pistol and scared them out. When our

81

friends heard about it, they said that was dangerous, so Willard got rid of the toy. Sometimes we'd have the tables set up for customers and a group of men would come, order soda and play cards. Willard finally got tired of it.

"I have a place to sell food," he said. "I'll be happy to serve any of you gentlemen, but you can't sit around and play cards!"

They were belligerant when they left and they didn't come back. Some of our good customers told us that the men were knocking us and the restaurant. It didn't bother us because by then business was booming. Soon we needed more space, so we stopped renting rooms and converted them to three upstairs dining rooms. We were amazed when famous entertainers booked in Milwaukee began to find the teashop.

THE FAMOUS CAME:
IRENE DUNNE, MAE WEST and FANNIE BRICE

So many stars began coming that I bought an autograph book. One night Willard rushed into the kitchen.

"Irene Dunne's out there!" he gasped. I ran to the door to look and there she sat, as regal as on the stage and in the movies.

"Bessie, you take over the overseein'," I said, whipping off my apron. (We couldn't stay apart for long—her divorce was final and she moved up here to be near me and work at the restaurant.)

"Where you going?" she called after me.

"Gotta get my new autograph book!" I ran out to greet Miss Dunne and ask if she minded signing her name.

"Not at all," she said. "It's my pleasure. Everyone's been telling me about this restaurant."

So Irene Duune was the first person to sign my autograph book. Fannie Brice came shortly after that. Some of the New York stars stayed overnight in one of our guest rooms that we quietly reserved for them. The woman agent who booked them was familiar with our place and a lot of the stars preferred it to a hotel.

After a couple of years somebody complained to the health department that we only had one bathroom, so we had a former servant's quarters turned into a bathroom for ladies. It was nicer, but we missed the lines and joking in the hall: "Your turn!"

Another time Willard ran all flustered into the kitchen.

"Who's out there?" I asked. I could tell by the way he acted, when it was someone special.

"Mae West! Mae West and her whole group!" he said.

"Mae West?" I said, flustered myself. "Did we have a big enough table?"

"Lucky enough, we did!"

I hurried to peek into the dining room. There sat Miss West, all prim and lady-like, not a bit like she was on stage.

"Lord almighty! I gotta get my autograph book!" I grabbed it and hurried out to meet her.

She wrote a verse that ended: "Next to home, this is best!/ Take my word,/ Mae West." Then she visited with us and gave us tickets to her show. We went, and afterwards we went backstage and talked to her. Mae wasn't lewd at all, but she made a lot of money portraying a hussy. They always made out that she was so buxom, but she wasn't. (You take Sophie Tucker—she was BIG! I saw her when she performed at the Majestic Theater. She was as big as Sammy Davis Jr. was little. He'd come to the Majestic with the Will Masterson Trio when I was an usherette.) Mae and her crowd came back for all her main meals and we had to save dinner until after her show was out.

Famous Negro singers came, too: Paul Robeson and Rollard Hayes.

One famous person from New York didn't sign my book. In '27 or '28, a well-dressed man was eating at an off-hour and began visiting. Then he introduced himself. "I'm Legs Diamond," he said, "and I'm runnin'!" He was supposed to be a material witness in New York for a famous murder case and he didn't want to testify, so he was running from the authorities. I suppose he was afraid of ending up at the bottom of the ocean with a weight to his ankle, but he out and told us who he was. Legs was on the lamb!

Almost half our trade came from Chicago. On Sundays and often during the week, cars from Illinois were parked up and down the street. We had the famous and the not-so-famous. One Chicago man had a Rolls-Royce he'd park in front of the restaurant. One man we called "Mr. Deusenberg" had a maroon town-car, a German-made Deusenberg, and he'd bring actresses. The chauffeur's livery was the same color as the car. Mr. Fisher, the druggist at the corner, told us that the car cost forty thousand dollars. When the chauffeur got out, he was always polishing it. Mr. Deusenberg was nasty because he made his black chauffeur come in the back door. The driver would walk through and sit in the main dining room, yet his boss made him come in the back door, but we didn't like it.

Discrimination was still around. We had a clean-cut black waiter who decided to get a sandwich at Wrigley's Restaurant on his day off. They didn't refuse him, but he had to wait and wait while they served other people. When they finally served him, he bit into a big lump of salt they'd put in his sandwich, so he walked out.

All the while we were dealing with people, our dog Pal was our constant companion. He'd be out and people'd come across the street to see him. And that dog was hard-headed—he wouldn't mind. He'd stand on the sidewalk and look this away and that away, then decide which way he wanted to go. So one day he was trotting behind the mailman and I said, "Hello, Pal," and he stopped and looked at me. I let him make up his own mind and he studied whether he'd go with the mailman or with me. I reckon he thought, "She feeds me—I'd better go with her!"

Everyday, Willard had to go to the First Wisconsin Bank on Twelfth Street and we didn't want Pal to go. So he'd sneak on the walk on the other side of the street until we were almost at the bank, then he'd run to us when we couldn't make him go back. I was crazy about walking in the snow and Pal'd come along, jumping over the drifts. If I could walk now, I'd do that yet! Then one year the city came up with a law that you had to keep dogs tied, so I kept Pal on a rope on the clothesline.

Pal had such a way with humans, even Mrs. Uihlein next door liked him. She was a white-haired, high-class German frau. We had plenty of help but I liked to work around the yard and in summers I'd get out and push the lawn mower. "You shouldn't do that," she'd say. "Let the men mow!"

She had a housekeeper, Theresa, who was from northern Europe and had worked for Uihleins for twenty-seven years. She went to church four times a day and she wouldn't let anybody help with her work. Mrs. Uihlein wanted men to do the snow and Theresa'd go out without boots, and shovel!

Those were happy years with good neighbors, Willard and Pal, and the glory days of my life with fine cars lining the streets and customers streaming in. The mayor, judges, doctors and lawyers. New York actors and actresses. It seemed that almost every actor or actress who came to Milwaukee had to have at least one meal at our place.

And sometimes numbers men came.

THE NUMBERS MEN

Two brothers who ran the numbers game in Chicago came on Sunday afternoons. One Sunday, a waiter came rushing into the kitchen.

"He gave me a thousand dollar bill—J. gave me a thousand dollar bill!" he panted. "What'll I do with it?"

"Take it back to him!" I said. "We haven't got that kind of money!" So the waiter went back and I peeked out the door to see what the man would say when he gave him his money back.

"That's the smallest I've got," the numbers man said and opened his wallet to show the waiter. To pay for the dinner, he turned to a friend and borrowed a hundred dollar bill.

A tall guy named Joe Biltry* had a Policy Wheel in Milwaukee. We'd all be working, then Joe Biltry would walk in and everything'd stop while we rushed to read the card to see if we'd caught a number.

"You ought to be ashamed of yourself!" Willard said to me good-naturedly. "You're supposed to be in charge of these people and you're right down there with them!"

It was true. I had fun right along with the kids when Biltry came. You could compare it to playing a football pool today. I caught fifty dollars in one day off the same number the first time I played. A waiter came and said, "C'mon, Mrs. Heard, pick a number."

"I don't know anything about it," I said.

"Just give me three numbers," he said.

"What numbers?" I said.

"Any numbers."

"Nine—sixteen—thirty-eight," I said, and forgot about it.

A few days later, the boy brought me twenty-five dollars.

85

"Beginner's luck!" everyone said.

"All right," I said, "put it in again."

That night the boy brought me twenty-five dollars. So a lot of the help started riding my number and I didn't get it anymore.

Biltry was a well-known gambler in Milwaukee and he owned property along Capitol Drive. Once in awhile he'd come into the teashop for a meal and he'd philosophize to the waitresses. "Don't worship money," he told them. "You'll never get anything if you worship money. Keep an easy grasp."

Once some of us caught a lot of numbers, but Biltry's money ran out and he couldn't pay.

"Everybody keep your numbers," Biltry said. Then he went down to Louisiana like he often did. Months later, a boy came into the kitchen with some money.

"What's that for?" I asked.

"Biltry paid off," he said.

Biltry was honest and paid his debts, but he was so superstitious, he wouldn't ride a Number 13 streetcar!

SEANCES

Often our friends visited in our private upstairs parlor. I didn't put chitlins on the teashop menu, but I made them. I never ate a chitlins until I moved to Milwaukee and I'd turned up my nose at them. Then after I ate some, you couldn't keep me away from them! Dr. Allen belonged to our dinner group and he always asked for them, so I'd fix them for him and they smelled so **bad**!

Dr. Rankford Holly and his wife, Ida, were leaders in our social group. He was a chiropractor, active on city boards—and psychic. He was deeply spiritual and active in the Unity faith, and about a year after the teashop opened we all decided to study with Dr. Holly. I must have been dying for spiritual growth; right away, I was interested.

One time we were meditating and Dr. Holly was reading petitions that we were supposed to repeat after him, then we'd meditate in silence on it. So he said something, then we said it. After awhile, there was a long silence and Dr. Holly didn't say anything. Finally Ida said, "Rank, you're asleep!"

Next we went into spiritualism, but I didn't care for that.

We had seances with this medium and his wife from the south side. The man had a trumpet and he had us all examine it before he began.

"Soon I'll go into a deep sleep," the man said, "and the trumpet will float around the room. If it stops in front of you, ask a question you want answered. Make the room as dark as you can." He nodded at me and sat down while Willard and I pulled the shades and turned out the lights. "Now one of you sit next to us and hold our hands," said the medium, "to satisfy yourselves that we don't touch anything while I'm in trance."

We all looked at each other and at first no one volunteered. I wasn't going to hold a medium's hand in the dark! Then attorney H____ got up. "Someone's got to keep them honest," he said, and walked over and sat between the couple.

The medium went into a trance and everything was so quiet I could hear someone's breathing. It went on for awhile like that, with the medium's head drooping like he was dead and us sitting in the dark, waiting for something to happen, when all of a sudden that trumpet started to lift up off the table like someone was picking it up! The medium and his wife were still by Mr. H____, but that trumpet sashayed up in the air and began floating all round the room. Then it stopped in front of me and I was so scared, I couldn't say a word!

Eva Jones was raising rabbits and when it stopped in front of her, she said real fast, "Am I going to have any luck with my rabbits? Am I going to have any luck with my rabbits?"

The medium was still in the trance when the lawyer pushed him with his foot, and the man jumped and opened his eyes. He was mad and the other people didn't like it, either. "What did you do that for?" someone said. "If you didn't want to take part, you shouldn't have come!"

My friend, Mrs. B___, wouldn't do anything unless she went to Mrs. Esser, this seer on the northwest side who advertised in the papers. I didn't believe anything in that woman! Willard and I went to her once and he was sitting in the room because he wasn't going to have me going alone to this place.

"Are you married?" she asked me. That was too much! My husband sitting there and she asked if I was married!

Another time when we were having a seance, Mae West was downstairs and she got so excited when she found out about it

87

that she told the spiritualist to wait until after dinner so she and her group could have one. So after dinner, Mae and her party went upstairs for a private seance. But she was shaking her head when she came back down to the dining room about an hour later. "They didn't tell me anything I didn't know!" she muttered. So she didn't tell the medium the line she was famous for: "Come up and see me sometime."

F.B.I. SCARES

We could have made a lot of money during Prohibition if we'd done underhand work. We didn't know anything about that, but one time someone had us get some good liquor to serve. We were scared because the head of the F.B.I. and his wife (she was from Dallas) came once a week.

"I like southern fried chicken!" Mrs. F.B.I. said, but we didn't serve it that way. We served our chickens by the half.

We had some other F.B.I. people come in from Minneapolis, but they always told us who they were when they came—I reckon they wanted to warn us. So we made one try with liquor and we were serving this thing called a "Willarege Special" for seventy-five cents, and you could sell it as fast as you could make it. We were careful who we served it to because we always had so many people in the dining room, like Judge Shaughnessy and the Waukesha County District Attorney.

When you're running a business you've got to stay on it, so we didn't go out often. One night we decided to go to a show and when we came back Bessie said a man named Ed Monroe had called and called. Willard had some liquor made by a guy who made good stuff that didn't make anybody sick, and Bessie was afraid that this Mr. Monroe was an investigator. We were back from the show and working when she came running into the kitchen.

"Willard!" she hissed. "He's back! I think he's F.B.I.!"

Willard rolled his eyes like he did when he was nervous. "I'm getting rid of it!" he said. He grabbed the handle of a cupboard so that the door flew open, grabbed some bottles of liquor in two sacks and rushed out through the dining room and upstairs to the bathroom. He locked himself in, opened the bottles and poured all the stuff down the toilet! Bessie was out front and later she said that Willard looked guilty as sin when he came downstairs. Mr. Monroe caught up with him in the dining room, and asked to talk to him in private.

"I'm going out of town," Mr. Monroe said, "and I hear you've got some good stuff—I'd like to stock up my supply before I leave."

He'd wanted to buy some liquor! And Willard had thrown all that money down the toilet!

One time when the dining room was full, a fellow came in who must've been half-drunk, he was so loud. **"Mr. Heard!"** he yelled, **"they tell me you make the best gin buck in the city!"** It scared us half to death, because we didn't know if any investigators were in the room. You never knew, during Prohibition.

Shortly after, Dr. Carhart from Columbia Hospital had a party of sixteen from the East side. Our former employers, Mr. and Mrs. Schultz, were with the group and we served them a special drink.

"I wouldn't do that any more," Dr. Carhart said later. "It isn't worth losing your reputation for."

So we quit. We had a lot of respect for Dr. Carhart's opinion, and some of those other episodes had scared us.

Tragedy struck in 1928. Mother had helped in the kitchen once in awhile, but she was still working full-time in the restroom at the Inner Urban train station when she got sick. She had a kidney condition and got ill while Dr. Shane was on vacation. Another doctor told me not to give her anything but rice and milk, and she loved to eat. She was so weak, she was in bed and I'd bring her rice.

"Please give me some food," she begged.

"I just can't do it, Mother," I said. "The doctor told me not to give it to you."

But, Lord, that was hard! I loved her so, it just about cut my heart out not to be able to give her decent food. She got so sick the doctor sent her to County General Hospital. When I went out to visit she talked and joked, but she never opened her eyes.

"They give me sauerkraut and wieners for supper!" she laughed. She was always full of jokes. But she didn't open her eyes.

I couldn't visit her as much as I'd have liked because I had to be in the kitchen, but Willard went everyday. He'd been there on Friday, September 13, 1928, when the telephone rang. One of the waitresses answered and got Willard out of the front. He took the receiver.

"You can't be talking about my mother!" he said. "I was just there talking to her..." There was a silence as he listened, then slowly he put down the receiver and turned to me. "Mother's dead," he said.

She was fifty-four years old. It hurt me, too, because I was just a country woman and she'd taught me a lot. But I thought Willard was going to lose his mind. We didn't think he'd be able to go to the funeral because he had a nervous condition: he would faint and fall down. He couldn't stand any kind of upset. But he did go. Octavia was buried from St. Mark's African Methodist Church. Shortly after her death, grandma went to live with Ollie, her other daughter. The following months were terrible, Willard was so depressed.

"Where's Willard?" someone'd ask.

"Out at the cemetery," I'd say. "Goes to mother's grave everyday."

Willard's depressions were bad, but business was still booming. When the stock market crash came in 1929, we were hardly affected. We didn't know that soon a Great Depression would change our lives.

10
Dreams Always End

We didn't know what Black Friday was when Walter Kohler Sr. was running for governor in the late Twenties and we had a political luncheon. Marie Kohler came to Milwaukee to drum up support for her brother, and was going to talk to a minority women's club that had booked the teashop for the occasion.

Marie Kohler was a refined lady with a good education, and there were a lot of professionals' wives in the club. The women came in their finest togs and everyone was jabberin' and puttin' on the dog when Marie Kohler arrived. A thin, old-time lady who "belonged to the sporting world" was to introduce Miss Kohler, who was at the head table. The sporting lady stood up and the women stopped jabbering.

"Girls, this is the stuff!" the woman shouted and sat down.

That was the introduction for Marie Kohler. The room was so quiet, you could hear the upstairs toilet flush. No one laughed that day, but they sure did talk and laugh about it for years after! Kohler won the election despite the luncheon.

We made a huge mistake then, when we were still going big. A man tried hard to buy our place and we wouldn't sell. Then Dr. Carhart and some other businessmen wanted me to run the kitchen at the Milwaukee Yacht Club.

"We've got a good business going," I said, and later I wished I'd taken the job because we had it awful rough during the Depression.

The ones who suffered the most loss were professionals and business people, like the ones jumping out of windows and off of housetops all over the country. They were wealthy, the kind of people who were our customers. We weren't hit too hard in '29 and '30. Money wasn't flowing as freely as it had earlier, but we were still going pretty strong.

About then, the Urban League asked me if we would take in a foster child. Lena was from the County Children's Home, a big house in Wauwatosa, west of the city. Children over sixteen couldn't stay there—they were supposed to find jobs by then. Lena was in her twenties; for some reason the home had kept her a long time. The county bought the clothes and things, but we provided room and board. We were one of the first minority families to take in a foster child in Milwaukee County.

Lena was a good girl and she helped a little around the house. She was with us about two years before she left to take a job, and later she got married.

By the early 1930's, the neighborhood was changing. Some of our customers' cars had been broken into, and our neighbors, the Rosens,* were moving. They called Mrs. Uihlein and tried to get her to move, too, but she called us up and said she told them she wasn't going any place.

Whoever got the Rosen property tore the house down and built a junkyard on the other side of our driveway and filled it with old cars. Then they built a fence about ten feet tall, and a lot of our customers talked about it. Some of them stopped coming because of the junkyard. The people who ran the junkyard set the old cars on fire and the blaze would go way up in the air. Each time, I called the fire department.

"Don't be afraid to call," the fire captain said. "Any time you need us, you call!" The fire department would come right away and make them put out the fire.

By 1932, times were bad. The teashop was nearly empty from morning to night and we had to let most of our help go. Half the property taxes in the city were unpaid in 1932. Things hit here later than in much of the country.

Then, in the middle of the Depression, my sister Jennie died. She was still living with mama and papa in Washington, Arkansas, and had been playing cards with friends and had eaten ham they thought made her sick. Doctor Quack* was treating her and he didn't know what was wrong. Jennie suffered a long time, then she died. (A white physician in Hope, Dr. Carrigen, treated black people particularly nice, and often he didn't charge them. Later, he told papa that if they'd called him, he would have come.)

Mama never could forgive Dr. Quack. He was white, but he'd come around and talk to papa on the porch, and mama didn't like his coming after Jennie died.

"Dr. Quack is a great man!" papa'd say. "He can make gas and water!"

In the North, winter was the worst because we couldn't heat the teashop anymore. Some people burned broken batteries to keep warm, and when a guy named Jim came with a carload of old batteries, we made a trade. I gave Jim meals, and he brought loads of batteries. They seemed to be made with tar or oil, and when we burned them in the furnace they made a good fire, but they stunk. Then somebody came by and said we had to throw out the batteries because they were a fire hazard.

Times were hard for students, too. A young man from Marquette asked if he could paint a picture of the teashop in exchange for meals. We said, "Yes," and he painted a beautiful picture that we hung above the fireplace.

We had two pianos—Willard's upright, upstairs, and another one downstairs. We couldn't afford to hire a piano player anymore, then a musician came in and asked if we'd give him food if he played the piano, so we had some live music even in hard times.

One day, a man who'd been a big lawyer came by. His feet were on the ground—his shoes didn't have bottoms! Willard gave him food, too.

Another time, a man who'd had a job at the Journal came by for something to eat. Willard hurried into the kitchen.

"Regie," he whispered. "Mr. S. is in the dining room. He's out of work, needs some food. Think you can put something together?"

"Reckon we'll just eat light tonight," I said. But as I set a place, I wondered if we'd have enough for our supper. We were already eating as lightly as we could.

Mr. S. thanked us over and over as he downed the food. "I was sure that if Willard knew I was hungry, he'd give me something to eat!" he said.

Folks knew Willard would do anything to help a person. So would I. It seemed like we couldn't help helpin'. And we did, for as long as we could. Even when we were scraping bottom,

on the East side and managed to find little jobs for twenty-five cents an hour. Sometimes at night when we were sitting upstairs in the dark, people came and flashed lights in the teashop windows to see what we were doing. It just broke our spirit.

Mabel Baylor knew I had time on my hands, and maybe she asked me to fill in for her because of that, or maybe she really had something else come up; Dr. Baylor's office was in the Chapman Building and she often had to help him. One day she called.

"Reg," she said, "I was supposed to go to Kohler with Mrs. King, but something came up. Could you go with her?"

"I'd like to—Mrs. King's one of my favorite people."

Mrs. King was a prominent Milwaukee philanthropist and her husband was with the Wisconsin News, the evening paper owned by William Randolph Hearst. She'd had luncheons at the teashop and I'd met her several times. So one of Mrs. King's friends drove us to Kohler and on the way, Mrs. King kept saying how much she'd like to fly. Herb Kohler had told her he'd take her up in his plane anytime she wanted to go, and she said she was sure he'd take us up because it was a sunny day. I was getting jumpy at the thought!

When we got there, we had lunch with one of the Kohler women and I settled down because she was telling us about the Kohlers' Austrian beginnings and how they'd started the plumbing business. Someone told us about one of their sinks: it hooked up to electricity and had a lid so water sprayed up and washed the dishes. I thought it was a wonderful invention! Then we looked at the grounds and all the flower beds, and I was just relaxing when Herb Kohler came and talked to us. Right off the bat, Mrs. King said she'd like to go up in his airplane! He said he'd take us, so we piled in a car and he drove us out to a field where he kept the plane.

I nearly fainted when I saw that flimsy cub plane! We got out of the car, the wind was blowing and my heart was pumping, I was so afraid! I was praying that something would happen so we wouldn't have to go up, when Mr. Kohler took us up close to the plane to look it over. All the while I was praying, and I noticed Mrs. King was kind of quiet.

"I'll take you up if you want to go," Mr. Kohler said, "but it'll be pretty rough up there today with this wind."

"It is breezy, isn't it?" Mrs. King said. "Maybe we'd better make it another time."

We went back home and I didn't go near Kohler again until 1985 when I was ninety-one and visited the new Design Center. I wasn't a bit nervous: nobody paid any attention to this old lady swinging along on a cane between the fancy whirlpools.

"Something's wrong with Pal," I said to Willard one day. "He's not eating and he's just laying around. Look at his eyes." We bent over him and talked to him and petted him, and he turned his head a little, but he didn't get up.

"I'll take him to the animal hospital," Willard said, gently picking up Pal. I'll never forget how mournfully that dog looked at me as they went out the door. The vet called later.

"I think your dog's got stomach flu," he said.

The next morning the phone rang, Willard answered, then came quietly to the kitchen.

"Pal died," he said quietly. He'd told the vet to cremate Pal and didn't say anything to me about it—he thought it would be easier on me—so I never saw my little dog again.

Then good things seemed to start happening. The return of beer in April, 1933, had brought the breweries back strong again by 1934. In Milwaukee, that meant jobs. By the end of that year, some of Roosevelt's programs seemed to be working. He froze the mortgages for one year and we'd applied for an HOLC loan. Finally, a letter came from Madison that it had been approved and all we needed was the city's approval, so we were full of hope when we re-opened the teashop in 1935. Some of our old customers had made it through the bad years and found out we were open again. Business began to pick up.

Just when we were getting back on our feet and were able to make payments to Mr. Katz (the man who held our mortgage), inspections killed us.

THE NIGHTMARE

We'd always been on good terms with the inspectors because we were clean and kept things up, but one day an inspector came and said we had to paint the kitchen, put on aluminum paint. The kitchen was clean, but we ran around, got the aluminum paint and painted the kitchen. About a week later, another inspector came around.

"You can't have this aluminum paint in here!" he said. "Who told you to put this stuff on? You've got to take it off!"

So we painted over the aluminum.

Then inspectors went after the greasetrap and the plumbing. Our house had a big greasetrap down in the ground, that Willard kept cleaned out. It had been approved by the city when we opened because it was a good one, then here comes this inspector and another man in the middle of the Depression and says we have to put in a new greasetrap. There we were, sitting in the middle of nowhere, with no means. How were we going to put in a greasetrap?

"We don't have money to put in a greasetrap," I said. The tables were set up nicely, with linens and china, because Willard kept the dining room in perfect order.

"Looks like you got plenty of trade," the inspector said, looking at the tables.

"Oh, they always keep it this way," the other man said.

I talked to them about the greasetrap and said we were waiting for the HOLC loan to be approved by the city.

"You don't have it yet!" the inspector said, and it sounded like a threat.

Then a Mr. Brown from the state came and had something to say about the plumbing.

"What's the matter with the plumbing here?" he said.

"We don't have a problem with the plumbing," I said. We went all over the house and checked faucets and toilets.

"I can't find anything wrong with the plumbing," he said. "They're not going to make a goat out of me!"

I didn't know what he meant. Then here comes a letter from the Association of Commerce saying that we were not eligible for the HOLC loan, that we didn't live on the place. Well, we did live on the place and we could have proved it. We always kind of looked after Mrs. Uihlein when she was alone, and she was going to sign an affidavit that it was our home. But my husband went down to city hall and must've got in a rage and thrown away all the papers. We didn't have anything to go by, after that.

Several people offered to finance us, but our spirits were so broken, I didn't want anything else to do with it. On top of everything else, we'd begun gettin crank phone calls in the middle of the night.

"Does Negroes own this place?" someone would say. "If they do, we won't come there!"

"I just work here," I'd say, and hang up.

When you've got all your money tied up, and you've got one pulling this way and one that way, your spirit gets broken. Then it happened.

Early in the spring of 1936, it was cold and we didn't have much heat. Dr. P. J. Gilmer's mother had come to call and we were sitting in the foyer, close to the radiator to keep warm, when the doorbell rang. I answered it and there stood a short, dark-haired man with a paper in his hand.

"Is your husband at home?" he asked.

"No," I said. "Step in and I'll close the door."

So the man came into the foyer and handed me the paper.

"This is a foreclosure notice," he said. "If you don't get out at once, I'll have the sheriff put you out." Then he left.

I was so shocked, it was like somebody'd hit me over the head. Mrs. Gilmer got up, embarrassed, excused herself and hurried out the door. When Willard came home, we didn't know what to do. We'd never been on welfare or anything like that, so we called Reverend Cecil Fisher, our minister at St. Mark's African Methodist Church. He and his wife came over right away and told us how sorry they were. He took it from there, and got somebody who'd store our furniture; the man from the storage company came the next day.

A few days later, the storage man came with a truck, and Reverend and Mrs. Fisher helped us pack all the china, silver and furniture. I wanted to leave the carpeting, but Reverend Fisher said, "No, take it up," so we did. It took us two days to get all that stuff in storage. The man at the storage company asked if there was something I wanted to keep, and I was lucky I didn't put in all of my silver. We stored almost everything but our bed, a lamp and table, a couple of chairs and mother's brass bed. We even stored the painting of the teashop—our only picture of it.

Fishers were highly respected, and true friends. We never lost their friendship until the day he died, almost forty years later. Reverend Fisher was working with Outdoor Relief, getting help for poor people, and he wanted to get us a room with some of their friends, but I wanted to go someplace to hide my head, I was so ashamed. Willard found a room in a boarding house that had been an Uihlein mansion, down the street on Fifth and Galena next to several other mansions that had been homes of the Uihlein brothers. They'd built them so they could be close to the brewery at the top of the hill. The boarding house had been a fine home, but now it was for down-and-outs, and when Willard told me where we were going to live, he wept. It was so humiliating, to go from the top to the bottom in one big swoop. Hurt. Anger. Bitterness. I felt them all.

To get aid, we had to apply for Outdoor Relief. Almost everybody on relief pulled coaster wagons to the building to pick up food, shoes, clothes. I'm thankful they didn't make me go down and sign. Willard must have been down at the office signing when the man came to cut off the heat, because Bessie and I were alone. It was April 29, the day before our wedding anniversary. After the heat was off and the man had left, we had our first laugh in a long time.

"I'm so glad they finally cut that off!" Bessie said.

"Bessie, what are you saying?"

"They been threatening for so long to shut off the heat," she said, "every time somebody walked up the front steps I was afraid they were going to turn it off. Now we don't have to worry about it anymore!"

We laughed and laughed. But Willard wasn't laughing when he got home from signing up for relief, and he broke down when we were alone. Toward night, the doorbell rang, I went down to answer it and there stood Mrs. Baylor with a big bunch of American Beauty roses.

"I couldn't forget your anniversary," she said. She had tears in her eyes. "I know I'm a day early." The next day would be our fifteenth anniversary and I almost cried right there, but I asked Mrs. Baylor in and found an ice bucket for the flowers.

"Come on to the kitchen for a sandwich," I said. "It's the only table left."

I fixed sandwiches and Bessie came down to eat with us. We did more talking than eating, then Mrs. Baylor left and I carried the roses upstairs.

The next morning, Bessie and I were packing the last of the dishes and the doors were standing open, when some young people stuck their heads in the doorway and laughed at us. It made the pain worse, because my dream had been to have a restaurant for our people. I was heartsick. Dr. Holly and Stanley Ward moved the furniture for us and had taken almost everything to the rooming house. Willard and Bessie had gone outside. I went upstairs to take one last look.

Slowly, I walked through the private dining rooms that had echoed with laughter and music. My footsteps were hollow on the wood floors. Everything was quiet, then I heard a muffled clanking outside and I looked out a window. A truck was hauling a wrecked car into the junkyard. I turned and walked into our bedroom. It was bare except for our bed and the American Beauty roses in the ice bucket, in the middle of the floor. I walked over, picked them up and went into the hall. My steps echoed as I passed the parlor bay windows where angels had bent over me.

I held the bucket of roses hard against my breast and stared straight ahead as I went down the steps, across the hall and out the front door. I never looked back.

11
Bad Program Until IBM

Bessie and I walked in front of Willard to the next block and up the steps to the boarding house. Rankford Holly and Stanley Ward were already in front, waiting with the furniture. I was like a zombie, not taking notice of anything except the sweet smell of the roses. Willard rang the doorbell and a big woman opened the door. Cabbage.

All I could smell was cabbage. Those smells—going from sweet roses to stale cabbage—have stayed with me all my life.

"Come on in!" the woman said. "I'm Mrs. Sorrel."*

I was in a daze as the owner of the rooming house led us upstairs to a large room with a fireplace, but I wasn't too dazed to see that everything was filthy.

"You get the finest room in the house!" Mrs. Sorrel boomed. "Finest and biggest! This was Uihleins' upstairs parlor. Can't use the fireplace—fire department's orders. You got an hour a day for kitchen cookin'. Y'all got any questions?"

"No," Willard said.

"If you need me, I'll be in my room." She waddled through the door ahead of Bessie, to show her to her room next to ours. Dr. Holly and Stanley set up our bed while Willard and I organized clothes. When they were through, they shook our hands and told us to call if we needed help, then they left. We didn't have any appetite to eat, but we put perishables into an icebox we were to share with a boarder, Mrs. Doe.*

In a few days, we found out that boarders stole food from the refrigerator. When we were lucky enough to be able to buy bacon, we could smell it frying and know it was ours, but not be able to prove it. We'd go into the kitchen, our bacon'd be gone and women would be sitting there, kersniggling. I got so I couldn't stand it, and there was no use talking to Mrs. Sorrel about it because she was in bed all day playing the numbers. She didn't do any work. She had a niece who tried hard to keep the house clean, but she couldn't keep up with it. I had a chafing dish, so I began cooking in our room.

Soon we had to go to bankruptcy court. It wasn't hard, because Attorney Hamilton was a personal friend and he made it easy for us. We'd always paid our bills and nobody appeared to put in a claim against us, so we weren't in court long. Later, Reverend Fisher talked to Mr. Katz, and he said he didn't know anything about the foreclosure notice on us and that he felt badly about our losing the restaurant. But there's a time for everything. I think our time had run out at the teashop.

We didn't have money to pay the storage company, and we asked if we could make installment payments, but the owner said, "No," we had to pay the whole bill. We didn't have the money, so we lost everything, even the painting of the teashop. About the only reminder of the glory days were some fingerbowls and a little silver. The rest was stored in our heads.

One night, Bessie's screaming and hollering woke us up.

"Oh, my God, what's wrong?" I said, running to the door. When I opened it, Bessie flung herself into my arms. She was hysterical, sobbing and trying to talk.

"Mama's dead! Mama's dead!" she cried and pushed a telegram in my hand. I scanned it: **"COME AT ONCE. YOUR MOTHER IS DEAD."** There was no name.

I felt as if I was being strangled. I handed the paper to Willard and grabbed our coats.

"Strange that telegram came from Louisville, Kentucky," Willard said as we hurried down the steps.

What were we going to do with no money? It was after midnight, so no streetcars were running. We hurried down to Wisconsin Avenue, then walked several more blocks to the telegraph office. On the way, we decided to try to call Miz Jo, a white lady in Washington who had a telephone. Only a few wealthy whites had phones. Miz Jo was really Mrs. Luke Monroe, wife of the congressman, but we knew her quite well. So when we got to the telegraph office, we asked the operator to call her. After a few minutes, the operator reached her and told Bessie to speak into the mouthpiece.

"Miz Jo, can you help us?" Bessie cried. "We got a telegram that says mama's dead!"

Miss Jo said something like "How awful!" and she hoped it wasn't true. She said she'd dress and go right over to our house, then telegram us. That's how good the white people were in Washington. We trudged back home, and hours later a telegram came from Mrs. Monroe: **YOUR MOTHER IS ALL RIGHT. MISS JO.**

We were so relieved, we were quiet awhile before we started talking, wondering how or why that first telegram came. We thought it might have been a foul trick. Shortly after that, Bessie went to Chicago to work, and I missed her something awful.

Willard had never done heavy work and, because he was on Outdoor Relief, he had to go out in the cold on a WPA project in Jackson Park. At night, he'd come home ready to drop.

"They've got us digging holes and filling them up, just to give us something to do," he said. Dig and fill. Dig and fill. That's all he'd do, because they were supposed to be working.

Mrs. Nicholson heard about us, and she called me back to work part-time at the Surf, but she was in trouble financially. As soon as I started work, Willard had to quit the WPA job because they wouldn't let two of us work—and each of us was only making sixty dollars a month! So Willard went looking for any kind of job for people he'd worked for before. But the worst was coming.

Wisconsin's winter of '36-'37 was frigid cold, and Mrs. Sorrel wouldn't have any fire. She had two furnaces and the men would go down and light some coal or batteries in the furnace to start a fire for their wives, then Mrs. Sorrel'd sneak down and put it out. We didn't have money for coal, but we'd burn old batteries in our fireplace when she wasn't looking.

Mrs. Sorrel had a houseful—the place was runnin' over with people—and everybody was paying sixty dollars a month for a room. She was making a lot of money, but she wouldn't furnish heat. And it was so cold, on the day that King George died it was twenty-five degrees below zero. Above us, in the attic she had cots for single men. They were lined up dormitory-style and they had little oil stoves they heated with. A man went out, got gasoline and put it in an oil stove, and it exploded.

"Fire!" someone yelled down the stairs. "Got a fire up here!"

"I'll get the fire department!" someone called.

So the firetruck came and I was thinking we didn't have to worry because the fire was upstairs. It was sixteen below zero and the water was freezin' as fast as the firemen were throwin' it up. We heard them clomping up the stairs and thought they were going to the attic, but a bunch of them broke into our room and started knocking out the ceiling! One threw canvas on our bed and the others began breaking windows. We had a beautiful lamp with a painted shield that had belonged to mama, and they threw it out a window. They threw most of our stuff out the window and we never got it back. After the fire was out, a fireman came and asked us to come down to the kitchen. He sat down and we sat down.

"Have you got insurance?" he asked. I didn't laugh then, but I'm laughin' now!

"We had to let it go," I said. I'd even let my life insurance go, and that was the most frightening thing in my life, when I didn't have any insurance. I'd seen people who had to be buried as paupers and I was scared to death that could happen to us. After we were working, as soon as I could, I bought insurance.

After the firemen left, water and ice was all over our floor, so Mrs. Sorrel moved us to a small room on first floor. In the next weeks, snow was piling up outside and we could see our breath inside. Seemed like our bones were full of frost! I began wearing my coat all the time and Willard wore a coat and high boots, and we took turns sleeping in the bed to keep warm. One day, I was shaking with cold and I got mad, real mad!

"I'm going down to see if there's any fire in that furnace!" I said.

I stomped down to the basement, pulled the chain to the lightbulb and peered around until I found our furnace. I was walking to it when I tripped on something and looked down. Heat ducts! I stepped over them, looked up at our furnace and saw black holes where pipes should have been. I looked down at the ducts on the floor again. **Our** heat ducts! Mrs. Sorrel had disconnected the furnace! I ran up those steps, down the hall and threw open her door—I didn't even knock.

There she was in bed, playing Policy! I don't remember what I said, but I'd never talked to an older person like that in my life.

"I'm going to get the police!" I shouted at the end and slammed out of the house.

It scared the devil out of her. But I didn't go to the police—I went to Dr. Holly's house and told them what happened.

"Regie, you and Willard come over here," Dr. Holly said. "You know you've got a place with us."

"Oh, we can't put you out—" I said.

"Friends can't put out friends!" Ida said.

They were twenty years older than we were, but we were close; they talked to me and I agreed that we had to move. By the time I got back to Mrs. Sorrel's, she'd run out and got a man to put the ducts back up, but we moved out. We left a lot of good stuff in that basement, like mother's brass bed, but I was so glad to leave I didn't miss them.

It was a hardship for Holly s, because they gave up their bedroom for us. We paid them rent and stayed about six months before we could afford a little apartment. Mrs. Baylor had an apartment next to Calvary Baptist Church and she told us about a vacancy downstairs. So we rented it. We had a living room, bedroom, kitchen and porch where we had a small icebox. And we had all the heat we wanted. You couldn't see in there for the heat!

Our landlord was an old man named Jones* who had an ice and coal place—sold ice blocks, and coal by the bushel. We were on first floor, they had a great big furnace and we almost had to open the windows, it was so hot in winter. We started off paying twenty-five dollars a month rent and when Mr. Jones raised it to twenty-seven dollars I was ornery about it.

Mrs. Jones was a short, fat woman from Louisiana, and built so big in back, it looked like there was a pillow back there! She was a Seventh Day Adventist, and we'd be sitting on the porch on Saturdays in summer when she came huffin' and puffin' out the door to go to church.

"I'm behind!" she'd say, and waddle down the steps.

"She sure is!" Willard would whisper.

She had a no-good grown son, Bill,* who lived with them. Bill sold coal for his stepfather and folks joked that when he delivered a ton of coal, he'd leave some in the truck and drop it off at the Jones' house—that's why we had so much heat. Because of her religion, Mrs. Jones didn't do anything on Friday and Saturday. Mrs. Baylor lived across the hall from the Jones. Dr. Baylor had died and left her pretty well off, but she'd started running with rich Chicago people and spent all her money, lost almost everything. Mrs. Jones began picking at her about cooking on Saturdays, so Mrs. Baylor'd come down to our apartment and eat. I just went on cooking and Mrs. Jones didn't mess with me about it, but she resented it. Once she said something to me about the heat or lights, so I spoke to her husband.

"I haven't said anything to you about anything, have I?" he said.

"No, you haven't," I said.

"Don't pay attention to nobody else then!" he said.

He made a good living, and his wife and Bill treated him like a dog. She wouldn't cook for him, but she'd cook pork chops for Bill. And she'd take Mr. Jones' money and give it to Bill. The Jones fought like cats and dogs. I don't know how she got the money in the Depression, but she went downtown one day and bought a fur coat for nine hundred dollars, and I thought they were going to kill each other!

"I want my money!" he yelled. "I want my money!"

We could hear them yelling about the coat and money, and Mrs. Baylor was listening to every word we couldn't hear, and later she told us what they said.

Mrs. Baylor was always going to psychics, and one day she wanted me to go with her to a woman psychic, and asked me to loan her five dollars. I didn't want to lend her the money, but I did. So we went to this place, climbed these dark old stairs and went into this room where a candle was burning in front of a woman with a rag tied on her head. That woman took one look at me and started yelling.

"Get out of here!" she shrieked. **"Don't you ever come here again!"**

It scared us and we ran. I didn't believe in what she was doing, and maybe she knew I was an unbeliever, or maybe she thought I was with the police.

The Jones' bathroom was over ours. She'd get up on Sunday morning to wash clothes, and their dirty water would run down into our bathroom. And anytime they'd flush, it would come up in our bathroom. So I called the health department, and an inspector came.

"Yah, you got a problem," he said and scratched his head. "But there ain't no law to make a man fix his property. You can move if you want to, but I'll speak to Jones."

Then the murder happened and we didn't live there much longer, so I don't know if anyone ever fixed the plumbing. One morning I was making breakfast, when I heard Bill going down to fire the furnace. I noticed how happy he sounded, because he was singing in the hall before he went to work. I'd never heard him do that before. Awhile later the police knocked on our door.

"Have you seen Bill Jones?" he said.

"Yes," I said. "He was here a little while ago—I heard him go down to tend the furnace."

"Anything else?" he said.

"I heard him leave—I suppose he was going to work."

"Did you notice anything else?" he said.

"Only that he was singing," I said. "Never heard him do that before. Is anything wrong?"

"Mr. Jones is dead—shot in the head," he said.

He'd been killed at his business, and the police took Bill and his mother down to court for questioning. Later, two boys were sent up for robbing and killing him.

Shortly after that, we moved to a lower flat on Fourth Street. Later, we heard that Mr. Jones left everything to Bill. Talk about retribution, people said that the poor woman really suffered, that Bill treated her bad and she didn't even have underwear to wear when she died. She went out on the street when she was old and cursed the day her son was born.

I was still working at the Surf, and Willard didn't approve of his wife supporting him. He was a proud man, so to keep him from feeling badly when I got my check, I'd have him cash it and handle the money. There were no jobs to be had, but God works in mysterious ways.

Heil was running for governor, and there weren't any

Negroes working at his company. That was the first thing they'd use against him in a election, and I think that's why they hired Willard. They'd had two women doing the work he did and they almost worked that man to death! He was going at five o'clock in the morning and he had to work half the night. Governor Heil didn't know anything about it, and one day he came into the factory.

"Mr. Heil! Mr. Heil!" everybody said, and they were all running around because he was there.

"Who are you?" he said to Willard. They talked and Governor Heil was nice. He probably wouldn't have believed it if Willard had told him that Mrs. Heil had been a customer at our teashop. The job was about to kill Willard and he couldn't take it any longer, so he quit.

By then we were getting ahead and had a nice apartment. I'd be at work during the day, but Willard must have been going through hell, running around taking any job he could find, when one day he saw the ad. It was a "help wanted" classified for a job at IBM. He'd never applied for anything like that, but he went over to IBM on Jackson Street. He was all smiles when I came home from work.

"Looks like you must've got a job!" I said.

"You are looking at 'Mr. Building Service'!" he said, putting his thumbs to the sides of his chest and pretending to swagger like a big-shot.

"Ooh, my!" I bobbled my head back and forth. "Sounds mighty fine!"

"It's a high-class name for a maintenance man. They said that way they can pay me higher wages—"

"How high?"

"Sixty dollars a month! I'll be in charge of maintenance and ordering supplies."

His going to work for IBM was the best thing that ever happened to us. It was small then and there was an art school in the same building. He liked his job, but after he'd worked there over a month, nobody had paid him.

"You better ask them when you're getting your check," I said.

"I don't like to say anything," he said. "It'll be coming."

So many things you don't know how to do, and he didn't want to upset anybody. Finally, after almost two months, a man from the office talked to him.

109

"Haven't you been paid yet?" he asked.

"No," Willard said. So they paid him.

We always thanked the day he saw that ad because he worked there twenty years, until he retired. After Willard had been at IBM awhile, sometimes we catered for his manager and his wife, the Martins, in Elm Grove. Later on, in the 1940's when papa was living with us, he was looking out the window when Mr. Martin came to pick me up to cater a lunch for Mrs. Martin.

"That's the only rich man I've seen since I lived in Milwaukee!" papa said.

Willard told Mr. Martin and he laughed. He was so good to us! Long after he retired, he wrote to us from Florida. You might say we ran with the big ones!

12
Gains and Losses

My sister Mozelle died toward the end of the Depression, and by 1938 papa was writing that he and mama weren't well. I knew I'd better go to Arkansas and wrote that I'd come soon.

"Hurry up and come," papa wrote back.

I was trying to figure out when I could go, when a letter came from one of the Tyus brothers saying people were stealing papa's fine old books from the house, and chickens and things from the garden.

"I better go down and see what's going on," I said to Willard. So I went to Washington in September, 1938, and was shocked to see how mama and papa were aging. The house was run down and needed paint. Papa must have had a light stroke, because he was dragging one of his feet. Worst of all, they were afraid.

"Never had to lock doors in all the years we lived here," papa said.

"Your daddy began to notice some of his books was missing," mama said.

"Some of my first editions," papa said. "We'd be in the back of the house and somebody'd go in the front and steal."

He looked whipped. That was the saddest thing I ever saw—proud papa, former deputy sheriff, admitting he couldn't protect his own house.

Mama's heart was bothering her, and she got short of breath when she was on her feet. I wondered how she'd managed to can the dozens of jars of fruit in the pantry.

"Looks like you canned for the whole town!" I teased.

"I try to keep busy," mama smiled, but the life was gone from her voice.

111

"Why don't we have some of these berries for breakfast?" I said. I opened a jar and it smelled funny, so I tasted the fruit. It had gone sour. Then I checked the others. They had all gone sour. Mama had always been careful about her canning, but I had to throw out all the fruit. I don't know if she didn't have sugar or if she'd forgotten how to can. I wrote Willard: "I have to bring them home."

He wrote a beautiful letter back and said that our home was theirs, to bring them. Because of the thefts, mama and papa had no compunctions about coming—they were glad to come. Papa'd never been to Milwaukee, but mama'd been up to visit two or three times when we'd had the teashop and had lots of room. I couldn't bring them right away because they had to break up housekeeping, so I helped mama sell as much furniture as we could and give the rest away. They had antiques, including the first bed they had when they were married. I did as much as I could, then I had to get back to Milwaukee. But mama was capable of selling.

"You come as soon as the house is sold," I said before I left. "Henry wants you to stop in St. Louis for a few days." We hadn't seen him in years, but I'd called my brother and he said he would send mama and papa fare to St. Louis. In November, Louie Tyus took them to the Hope depot and put them on the train. Henry had sent the money and they went to St. Louis for about two weeks. Bessie sent the fare to Chicago, where she was living, and helped them change trains to Milwaukee. We'd sent fare for the trip from Chicago to Milwaukee.

But mama had quite a bit of money when they got here. That smart little old lady had sold the house and things and saved the money.

Willard and I had a very small apartment on Fourth Street, so we gave mama and papa our bedroom and slept on the couch. I brought them up here and they didn't know anybody. Lord, I wouldn't make that mistake again! In Washington, nobody had paid any attention to mama's not having her right arm. Up here, city people would look at her like she was a freak, and it hurt her. She'd lost her physical arm almost eighty years before, but she said that hand was always there. "I can feel those fingers itchin'," she'd say.

Mama never quit working in the South, and when I brought her here I didn't let her do anything because I thought she was too sick. That was a mistake: she began to get fat. Maybe she would have, anyhow, because there wasn't much room to walk around in our apartment. But we had plenty of heat and money coming in, with Willard at IBM. We even had a New Year's Eve party that year.

Our friends were looking out for us during those years, especially Hollys. They'd been in their fifties when they adopted baby Joanne,* and she was a teen-ager, so Rankford and Ida must have been near seventy the summer of '39 or '40. Because of them, I was aware of a higher power in my life. One night that summer, we'd gone to bed on the couch and our window was open, and Ida Holly came to the porch window.

"Reg?" she said.

"Yes, Ida?" I said.

"Mr. Jackson has a house up the street he wants to rent—would you be interested?"

"Would we!" I said.

A couple of days later, Mr. Jackson and Mrs. Jackson came and talked to us.

"We've got a three-bedroom house I'd like to rent you," Mr. Jackson said, "at 424 West Vine."

"What are you charging?" I said.

"I've been getting forty dollars," he said, "but you can have it for thirty."

We took it, and shortly after we moved, the Children's Home asked us to take two sisters as foster children. Ora and Hazel were cousins of Lena, the foster daughter we'd had at the teashop. The girls were school-age and had an older sister, Mabel, but we only had room for two in a small room off the kitchen. So I went to Dr. and Mrs. Holly.

"I know it's asking a lot, but this girl needs a home," I said. "Would you talk to the social worker?"

So the Hollys took Mabel. The girls' mother was one of the nicest people I ever knew. "Now, you do what Mrs. Heard tells you!" she'd tell them. Rebecca was another daughter (she became Billy Bruton's maid later and went to Detroit). She'd visit Ora and Hazel.

"Acts like she thinks she belongs here, too," mama'd say. "If she wants anything, she comes to you—"

"—like that pair of shoes she needed," I laughed. I had a lot of fun with them, and Ora was a wonderful girl. I had a big vase and one time Ora was trying to clean the blinds for me. She accidently knocked the vase over, broke it and was sure I'd be mad.

"Why should I be mad," I said, "when you were doing something so nice?"

Ora was always finding things to do and liked to start supper on days when I was working, so she was a big help. Mama and papa loved the girls, too.

LINCOLN HOUSE NURSERY SCHOOL

I was working at the Surf when two young women from State Teachers College came to see me.

"You've been recommended by the Urban League for a new position," one said. "Would you like to work part-time with a dietician at a nursery school, a government pilot project?"

"It sounds interesting—business is slow here." I hesitated. "How much does it pay?"

"How does ninety dollars a month sound?"

"It sounds like I'll take it!"

The nursery school was sponsored by the State Teachers' College in the Urban League building on Ninth Street, in a brick building that had been a Jewish center. It was called "Lincoln House." It was a big step down from the teashop, but it was nice for the children: they got two meals a day. People on Outdoor Relief could bring children who were between two and four, and we had black and white in the school. The parents had to bring them and call for them. It was kind of a training program because some of the poor kids didn't know how to eat with a spoon. The dietician was a young girl and we did the buying and ordering. I had a woman who worked under me as a cook.

One of the two- or three-year-old boys was so allergic to eggs, he didn't have to see an egg: he'd know when an egg was around! We couldn't put egg in the custard or he'd scream and cry. Come to find out, his mother had fed him too many eggs when he was a baby.

At home, I was fixing meals for the family, then running to work, so Ora began to start supper. But Hazel had an emotional problem and cried all the time. And because I wouldn't let mama work, she was getting fatter. I thought it

114

was my place to take care of her, she'd done so much for me.

"Your mother's getting awful short of breath," Willard said.

"Heart trouble runs in the family," I said and tried not to worry, but everyone noticed that mama was getting more and more frail.

URBAN LEAGUE CAMP

When money was running out for the nursery school project, my pay was cut from ninety to seventy dollars, so I took a job at the Urban League's summer camp for underprivileged children. I arranged for Willard's Aunt Ollie to take care of mama, papa, Ora, Hazel and Willard, and for three summers I cooked and helped run the camp south of Milwaukee, near the government's model city of Greendale. The camp was under Roosevelt's National Relief Administration, and I was paid by the N.R.A. as a special supervisor. I worked with Comer Cox, an assistant to William V. Kelley, executive secretary of the Urban League—we called him "Kelley."

The site was chosen because there were barracks and beds from an old C.C.C. camp, and for the first part of the summer, boys from nine to twelve came, then those from twelve to sixteen. I was the only woman, so they let me bring a female guest until the girls came. I had Idean Kern visit a lot—her husband, James, had been head of the Urban League before Mr. Kelley. Mr. Cox was in charge of the boys and had a young man who assisted him and stayed at the camp. Mrs. Turney was in charge of the girls; when they came for the third and fourth sessions, I got to see my family because I went home every week-end.

"We've got enormous amounts of food at camp, the best of food," I told mama and Ora. I'd helped mama to a chair in the kitchen while we fixed supper. "I do the planning, ordering and buying—"

"What does Mr. Cox do?" mama said.

"He brings the food out and helps direct the camp. You should've seen the kids that first morning!" I laughed. "I almost came home! I got up early and hurried to the kitchen. I was pourin' dozens of cups of orange juice, stirrin' a huge kettle of oatmeal, makin' toast in the oven and buttering it."

"Sounds almost like me when y'all was little," mama chuckled. She liked to reminisce about Arkansas and she never said, but I knew she was homesick.

"I was so happy about feeding those kids their first meal away from home, by the time the boys filed in, I had breakfast out on the tables. Then I stood at the end of the dining room with Mr. Cox, to watch them eat."

"Bet they piled into that food," mama said.

"I wish! One by one, they took a bite or two, then put their spoons down and stared at their plates or laps. I couldn't understand it. 'They're not eatin'!' I told Mr. Cox. 'Why aren't they eatin'?' Know what he said?" Mama and Ora shook their heads. "'They're used to going to the store for a bottle of pop and a piece of bologna for breakfast.'"

"I like pop and bologna," Ora said, as she ran cold water on the potatoes.

"Won't give you the oomph you need, won't stick to your ribs," I said. "Poor little kids, I just kept makin' toast and oatmeal and after a few days, they'd tie into breakfast like lumberjacks!"

"Should've seen 'em when I went to pick her up today," Willard said from the doorway. "They all came running, yelling 'Don't take her away!' And when we drove off, they waved and yelled, 'Bring her back!'"

I reckon they knew how much I loved them, that's why they loved me. When I wrote a food report at the end of the third summer, the director of the N.R.A. said it was going to be kept in their archives in Madison.

TRANSITIONS

Gradually, mama was in bed more, and I took meals to her. She could sit if we helped her to a chair, and one day she was visiting with a friend and me.

"I had a dream last night," mama said. Her dreams were important to her, and mine are to me. "I saw myself flyin' through the air with a black dress on."

"Mama, you're gonna be scarin' your company away."

"Can't help what the Lord gives me to dream," mama said. "I'm not afraid to die..."

My friend and I tried to laugh it off, but I wondered about

116

the dream. The next day was March 10, 1941: Ora's birthday. Company was in the living room with papa and me, next to the library. Mama and papa had the bedroom off the library. We were visiting when I heard a little noise, so I went into mama's room to see how she was. She must have tried to get up because she'd fallen across the bed. I ran to her and she was still warm, but I knew she was dead.

Then I had an experience I'll never forget. My insides felt like they were an umbilical cord being torn out, being pulled, just tearing and tearing through by navel. Afterward, I felt a great emptiness. I've never had that happen when anyone else I loved died. Not Bessie, not Willard. Just mama.

I called for help and papa came.

"Get something warm and put to her heart!" he said, but it was too late.

My mother was eighty-two, over seventy years removed from her slave days. Rayner's was the first Negro funeral home in Milwaukee, and that's where the service was held. Willard shaved papa and cut his hair for the funeral, like he always did. They loved each other so, people thought they were father and son. But papa was so lonely after mama died, even Willard couldn't lift him.

"If I could only get a job," papa'd say, and he'd dust and sweep around the house and do anything to keep busy.

I walked around like I was in a trance, I was so lonely. When I wanted her badly, mama was always there. I didn't see her, but I could feel her presence.

A few months after she died, I bought a hardwood bedroom set with a twin bed at a secondhand furniture store on Third Street and had it delivered for papa. I'd fixed up his bedroom and put up new curtains, but I was grieving for mama and not paying attention to what was going on around me, so I didn't notice that papa was looking kind of raggedy. One day he said, "Reg'na, I don't like to complain, but those bugs are eating me up! Can't you do something about them?"

"What bugs are you talking about?" I said.

"In the new bed," he said.

I tore into that bedroom, ripped back the covers and, Lord, bedbugs were flying all over that bedframe! They'd come from the secondhand store. I threw out that mattress and bought a new one, but before we put it in the bedroom I spent days boiling bedding and scrubbing all the furniture.

117

All that year I kept thinking of mama and calling for her in my sleep, and one night I had a dream:

Bessie
was on one side of a bed
and I
was on the other
and mama was saying
"Bessie has to go on the other side."

I couldn't understand what the dream meant, so I tried to forget about it. Bessie had been having female problems and had gone to a doctor for tests. She was frightened of anything medical and when the doctor said she should have surgery, she came to get my advice.

"Bessie, you have to make your own decision," I said. I'd been putting off going to a doctor about an old fibroid tumor I had, and it wasn't my place to tell my sister to have an operation when I was afraid of one myself.

Bessie decided to have the surgery and she came through it fine, but we didn't want to worry papa, so I didn't tell him she was in Milwaukee Hospital. I went there twice a day to see her, and she was scheduled to come home on a Monday.

I was tired from doing the wash, but that Saturday night I pushed myself to the hospital with Ruby Stitt, a friend. It was August 18, 1942. Ruby and I were laughing and joking with Bessie, when all of a sudden she grabbed her head between her hands.

"I've got an awful pain in my head!" she said, then she was quiet. Those were Bessie's last words. I called the nurses, but she was dead. Of all the tragedies in my life, I think that Bessie dying from a bloodclot hit the hardest. I was walking around like a zombie again, doing things and not knowing I'd done them. Papa was so confused and upset when I told him Bessie was gone, it was pathetic to see and I knew what a mistake we'd made, not telling him that she was sick.

After the reality of Bessie's transition hit me, I remembered the dream and understood what mama was trying to tell me: Bessie'd gone to the other side.

* * *

"Ida, I don't know what I'd do without you and Rank," I said to Mrs. Holly one day when I was feeling low. We were sitting in her living room.

"We feel the same about you and Willard, Reg."

"Seems like everyone I love is dying."

"You've had a lot of losses—"

"Don't know where I'd be without you—been almost ten years since you and Rank taught me to look for Light inside myself."

"It's hard to see it right now, isn't it?" she said.

I nodded, but I couldn't talk, and Ida reached over and put her hand on mine.

The next year we suffered together. Dr. Holly had advanced cancer and we knew he was dying when he went in the hospital. One day Ida called me.

"Reg, they want me to come to the hospital," she said. We both knew what it meant. "Will you go with me?"

"Of course, Ida," I said.

When we got to the hospital we could hear Rank hollering, kind of yelping in pain. We went in the room and he looked so grey and frail, but he was fighting so hard, I hurt for him. He opened his eyes.

"Reg, what are you doing here?" he said.

"Oh, I just decided to come with Ida," I said, trying to sound light about it. He was suffering so, he couldn't help moaning. Ida was standing back, afraid, so I walked over to him, touched his forehead and closed my eyes, then Dr. Holly closed his eyes.

"Sleep, Rank, sleep," I kept saying softly. "Sleep, sleep, sleep..."

And he slept away right then.

The next day I was in his bedroom helping Ida pick out a suit for him for the funeral, and I don't know why I did it, but the closet door was open and when I was looking at Dr. Holly's clothes, I hugged his suit in my arms and all of a sudden—so help me God!—**he hugged me back**! I felt a warmth, and afterwards I was just filled with peace—that's the only way I can describe it. Somehow, Rankford Holly's spirit was there and that spirit had hugged me!

Chiropractors didn't make much money then and Rank didn't have insurance, so Ida was left almost penniless. She was proud, but a few weeks after the funeral I said, "Come on,

Ida, I'll take you down to the courthouse to apply for Old Age Pension."

It was the heart of World War II and cabs were hard to get, so we took a bus. At the courthouse, they treated us kind of shabby and we waited and waited. Ida was in her seventies, had bad heart trouble, and seemed sick. I was worried, but finally they took care of us. Ida was weaker and sicker by the time we left and there were no cabs around, so we walked to Seventh and Kilbourn to wait for a bus. She was worse and worse, I was scared and no bus was in sight.

"I'm going to thumb for a car!" I said and Ida didn't object, she was so sick. So I did something I'd never done before and never did since: I stepped out in the street and put out my arm to thumb a ride. Before long, a car that had passed us stopped up the block and backed up.

"I told my husband it looked like that lady was in distress," the black woman in the car said as we got in.

"She is," I said, and told them Ida's address.

"I have a sister who lives in that block!" the woman said, and when we pulled up to the duplex where Ida lived, the woman said, "This is where my sister lives!"

Her sister lived downstairs from Mrs. Holly!

THE WRONG PAYCHECK: SEX DISCRIMINATION

Women were working in industry for the war effort and making good money. I was always trying to make money, so I took a job at A. O. Smith in about 1943. Before Willard and I went to work in the morning, I'd make breakfast for him and papa. Mrs. Daniels, the lady who rented the upper part of our duplex, fixed lunch for them. Willard came home from IBM for lunch because it wasn't far, and he'd visit with papa.

But after mama died, papa was lonely. He'd sweep the walk and yard until he almost swept off the grass, and people complimented us on how nice the place looked. And he'd pack around a dustcloth and dust all the time. He had the realization that he had to keep busy.

Meanwhile, I was busy at A.O. Smith. It was run over with officers from the armed services and, ooh, the noise! Sometimes I couldn't hear, and there was steam all around. I sat at a table with women, and men brought us parts for

B-17's. Some of the parts we painted, and some of them we oiled—screws for the tails of the B-17s. Then we wrapped them in color-coded paper. What we worked on went overseas.

I was over-punctual, worked fast, and the supervisor'd say, "Don't work so damned fast! Get up and go up on some of the other floors and look around!" But I didn't.

A. O. Smith had a nice reputation—they still do—and I liked working there, but they discriminated against women. Women did the same work and had the same hours as men, yet they got different pay. All the companies did it. Legally, my name had been "Reginald" ever since Mattie Royston gave me the idea over thirty years earlier, so it was "Reginald" for work records. The first time I got paid I got this big check. I didn't say anything and didn't cash it, but I took it home and showed it to Willard.

"What am I going to do with this?" I said.

"Hang on to it!" Willard said.

A few days later a man came up to me in the plant and talked to me about the over-payment. "Your name got in the men's file by mistake—Reginald's not too common a woman's name," he said. "You can keep the check, but we'll deduct the over-pay from the next one."

So the next check, they cut it off. The name of "Reginald" had been in the men's file and I'd been paid a man's wages. When they found out I was a woman, I wasn't worth as much! I'm glad that's changing now.

Some of the women worked like men, pitching and catching this molten stuff. And some of them had to get out the tools and collect the tools. A lot of men were working piecework and they didn't want to give up the tools when it was time. One day, a woman was trying to collect them and a white man wouldn't give them up.

"You black son-of-a-bitch!" he yelled.

And she hauled off and laid him out with one of the tools she was carrying! They had a meeting about it and fired the man. Everything was straight at A. O. Smith.

Those were years of big change, not all good. The men were in the army, the women were in the factories, and a lot of them were going to taverns after work and having a big time—the children were taking care of themselves. We'd tell jokes while we worked, and everyone at our table'd always be laughing. Then they were closing that plant and it was kind of

121

a feather in my cap because I'd decided to leave and they asked me to stay.

"We'll get you a job at the main plant on Prospect Avenue," my supervisor said, so I went there and talked to a man.

"We'll give you a new job," he said.

"I'd like to, but my father lives with us and he needs someone with him," I said. "I'll have to think it over." I was worried about papa. I think loneliness played a big part in papa's going down. His hearing was impaired, so I told him not to answer the phone when Ora was at school and he was home alone.

"Don't ever let anyone in when you're alone," I said. "This neighborhood isn't safe anymore."

"Don't worry—I won't let nobody in," he said.

One night after we were home and papa was in bed, Mrs. Daniels came down to talk to us. "Your father must have decided to try to answer the telephone today," she said. "He couldn't understand what the caller was saying, so he left the phone off the hook."

"How do you know that?" I asked.

"The police were here," she said.

"The police?" Willard and I said at the same time.

"The operator got concerned and called the police," Mrs. Daniels said. "Two policemen came and knocked on your door, but your father didn't answer. Then they peeked in the windows, but they couldn't see him, so they rang my doorbell and I came down. I knocked and called and finally got your father to open the door."

"Thank heavens!" I said.

"The police were real nice the way they talked to him," she said.

Papa was so ashamed he never told me about it, and I never said anything to him about it because I didn't want to embarrass him. By then I was mulling over the job A. O. Smith had offered me.

"I can't leave papa alone anymore," I said to Willard. "I'm not taking the job at the main plant." I didn't tell him that I hadn't been feeling well, either.

"We're making out fine," he said.

"I'll give notice tomorrow," I said.

So I did, and everyone seemed glad to have me home. About that time, Ora graduated with honors from North

Division. She became a fine woman and after she married, she came to see me and brought her children, five or six of them, all lined up on the couch. Hazel'd got so she wouldn't go to school, and the social worker moved her to another home where the woman kept her kind of like a pet—just dressed her and fussed over her—but Ora stayed with us. The Children's Home had my name on file and they'd call me to take short-term foster children over the years.

One girl I never thought I'd have as a foster child was Joanne, the Holly's daughter. She was seventeen or eighteen when Ida died—I think it was 1944, about a year after Rank died. Reverend Fischer was doing social work, and he and Mrs. Badger didn't want Joanne living alone. They couldn't get her to go anywhere else to live, and then they asked, "Do you want to live with Mrs. Heard?" and Joanne smiled big.

Because of her age, I had to go to court with Joanne before I could be her foster parent, but she was so scared when she went before the judge, she couldn't talk! He was kind and asked if I was a relative. I was afraid they wouldn't let Joanne come if I didn't say "Yes," so I lied: I said I was Mrs. Holly's cousin, and Joanne moved to our house.

I was glad to be able to help anyone I could, but my energy was dwindling and my weight was bothering me. Back when we had the teashop, a doctor had discovered that I had a fibroid tumor about the size of an orange. "It's not serious—we'll keep an eye on it," he'd said. Then we lost everything and I didn't have money for doctor bills, so I didn't have it re-checked. By '44 or '45 I was having some trouble, and I'd gained so much weight I looked pregnant. So I went to see Dr. Carhart and told him I thought that the fibroid might be acting up.

"My God, Reg, you've got a tumor in there!" he said when he examined me. "Why'd you let it get so big?"

"The other doctor said to leave it alone," I said.

"Who the hell told you that?" he said. He was really upset, and said he'd make arrangments for me to go into Columbia Hospital as soon as possible.

After I got home I stumbled into our bedroom, sat on the edge of our bed and cried, I was so scared. Since Bessie's and Rank's deaths I'd developed an awful fear of hospitals. Tl. next day, Dr. Carhart called and said Columbia had a room for me. "I told them to give you a nice private room," he said. That was an understatement! That room was so fine, when Dr. Carhart saw it he said, "I told them to give you a private room, not a hotel suite!"

Dr. Carhart was so kind and had such an aura about him, I think he was an advanced spiritual being.

"Everything'll be fine," Willard said, but I saw fear in his eyes, too, and when they put me on that cart and rolled me to the operating room I was sure I'd never see him again in this dimension.

But I did or I wouldn't be telling this story. And I was a lot thinner when I saw him. No wonder I'd looked pregnant: the tumor was the size of a baby—seven pounds!

13
Traveling with Age

The first time we rode in a car to Arkansas was in 1946. Papa was ninety-two years old; it was his last trip home.

My niece, Letha (Minnie's daughter), and her husband, Walter, came from Chicago to get papa, Willard and me. After the war, cars, tires and gas were in bad shape, but Walter had a cab company and a new Buick taxicab.

It was the middle of summer, so hot that we decided to leave late to beat the heat, so we left about five o'clock in the afternoon. Willard sat in front with Walter, and Letha, papa and I sat in back. After we finally got through Chicago, it started getting dark.

"Stop the car! Stop the car!" papa yelled, about halfway through Illinois. It scared us and Walter stopped, but papa couldn't tell us why he'd been frightened. We thought maybe he had a premonition. We started up again and soon papa was saying, "I can't see nothin' ridin' at night!"

After we'd driven a few hundred miles, Walter pulled to the side of the road to rest. We thought papa'd go to sleep, but he didn't close his eyes and I don't think anybody went to sleep. I couldn't sleep sitting up, thinking about someone coming and hitting me over the head!

The car was new, but the gas was bad and after Missouri we had sand in the gas tank. Then we had to stop often so Walter could clean it out. He tried to borrow something at a filling station to clean out the sand, but the attendant wouldn't let him have a tool. The guy wanted to clean it, and he wanted so much money!

At the next filling station, the guy left the cap off the radiator. We'd go a while and the water'd start boiling out.

Walter stuck a rag in, but it didn't quit. We had to go a ways and stop, go a ways and stop. But we had fun! Papa and I sat on Walter's straw hat and mashed it. Then we sat on papa's hat. Papa was kind of childish and every time he sat with his head hanging over the front seat, I'd kind of scold him.

"Let grandpa alone!" Walter said. "Let grandpa alone!"

It started raining, we got to the start of a long hill and there was a big Greyhound bus right on our tail. And papa stood up! What made it so funny, Walter had been on papa's side all the time, but when papa stood up, Walter boiled over.

"Sit down, Grandpa!" he yelled. **"You're gonna get us killed!"**

What with all the stopping, it took a long time to get to Helena, Arkansas, where my sister Minnie lived. She and her family lived on a hill at the edge of town and there wasn't much of a road. We made sharp turns in the dark, rounded the last curve, and pulled up to Minnie's. We all jumped out of the car, except papa. Papa wouldn't budge.

"Come on, Papa!" I said. "We're at Minnie's house."

"I don't want to go to the poorhouse!" he said. "I don't want to go to the poorhouse!"

He thought that we were taking him to the poorhouse. He knew he was old, and he had memories of the poorhouse on the road to Columbus. You never can tell what an old person is thinking about, but I felt so embarrassed. Minnie came out to meet us and there was papa, not wanting to get out of the car.

"I'm not goin' to no poorhouse!" he kept saying.

Minnie slid on the seat beside him. "Papa, it's Minnie!" she said. "Don't you know me? I made some cornbread, just for you." Papa just looked at her, but she kept talking and he kept listening, and finally he inched his way out.

We stayed in Helena about ten days. Minnie and I'd grown apart over the years because she had nine children that took all her time and neither of us could travel, so we had a big time catching up on our lives.

Helena was right off the Mississippi River and every day it looked like a big storm was coming and we'd sit on the hill and watch it come.

"If you bury an ax in the tree the way the storm's comin', it'll turn it away," papa said.

"Minnie, get the ax!" I laughed when we saw a storm

126

coming. Sometimes papa'd chuckle, too, but most of the time he seemed serious, like he was in another world. All the while we were at Minnie's, he kept saying, "I want to go back to Milwaukee, Wisconsin!" He never left off "Wisconsin!"

Sometimes when we were watching the clouds boil up, we'd talk about the lynchings that hit around Helena about the time of the First World War. So Aletha and I were thinking about how the town used to be when we went shopping at a grocery store. It was crowded and I was pushing right up to the front and Aletha said she was shakin', she was so scared. But the clerk waited on me and everyone was fine.

Walter had cleaned the sand out of the tank and one evening we left for Washington. Minnie went, too; it was the first time she'd gone back in all the years she'd been married—almost forty years. We were driving along through West Helena and all at once Walter pulled off the road. On each side of the car there was a white motorcycle policeman.

"Where y'all goin'?" one said.

"Washington," Walter said.

"Everybody get out of the car!"

There we were, with papa ninety years old, but they made us get out of the car and we were shaking with fear.

"What y'all doin' around here?"

"Visiting my wife's people," Walter said. He had all these licenses on his car because it was a taxicab.

"Let me see your license!"

Walter handed him the license and they looked at it.

"Who does this car belong to?"

"I'm visiting my sister and mother-in-law," Walter hedged.

"Who does she work for?"

"They work for Mr. Stevens," Walter said. He knew that Mr. Stevens was a rich white man and the police weren't going to bother Mr. Steven's Negroes. Right then, the policemen let us get back in the car and go on through. Papa'd had good sense through the whole thing. He didn't say a word. He knew more about that than we did.

Down near Washington we got onto a little road, and met a colored man with a team of mules. He looked in the window as we passed him, and he turned around and came up to us and said to papa, "Aren't you Professor Robinson?"

Papa said, "Yes, yes!" and he was so pleased. They'd always called him "Professor" because he'd taught. Papa was an old

127

man, and that man remembered him.

The closer we got to Washington, the stranger it felt, because it was the first time we'd been there without mama. And the road had been changed so that we passed behind our house, but nobody seemed to notice it except me. The house was sitting between two fine houses that had been built on lots papa had sold off of our land.

"Papa and mama should be there," I thought, and wiped my eyes. If papa noticed, he didn't show emotion.

Washington had changed, with concrete walks all over. I'd written to my cousin Gert that we were going to stay one night; she was the daughter of Uncle Richard who'd done all the barbecuing. We got to her house, and then I don't know if it was the hot weather or what, but Letha got sick and I got sick, and it looked like Gertie was never going to get dinner ready. I guess she was too excited, so I had to cook the dinner, sick as I was.

Sunday morning, papa wanted to walk into church and surprise everybody. We were sick and for some reason Walter didn't want to take him. Papa was up bright and early, all dressed and starting to walk out the door.

"Where you goin', Papa?" I asked.

"Church," he said. "It's Sunday. Always go to church on Sunday."

"It's over a mile!" Minnie said. "And it must be a hundred in the shade!"

"Papa, you can't walk in this heat!" I said.

We wouldn't let him go, so papa didn't get to go to church and I've always felt bad about that. We should have arranged some way for him to go. We went into town afterwards, and visited. Mr. Haynes owned the hardware store, and they were so nice, Mrs. Haynes was kissing me.

"I never thought a white woman'd be kissing you!" Minnie said later.

Word spread that papa was in town and some people came to see him, so that made him happy.

The town was still famous for watermelons and when we left, Walter tried to take every melon they had. He had watermelons in the car and in the trunk, and we were straddlin' melons all the way home!

Going north, we stopped in North Little Rock for gas and Walter asked the white owner of the station if he could have the key to the bathroom. We could see the man say something, then Walter's face got long and he came trudging back to the car.

"He told me I could use a washrag," Walter said. We drove all over until we finally come to a colored area. We stopped in front of a house, and Letha and I went up and knocked. A woman came to the door.

"Lady, will you let us use your washroom?" we asked, and she let us use her bathroom. That's how southern Negroes helped out traveling Negroes.

We went on, and up toward Missouri we had the first blowout. We had to sit under a tree on the side of the road while Walter rolled the tire I don't know how far up the road until he got someplace where he could have it mended. A couple of hours later he rolled back the patched tire and we were on our way. Then we had another blowout!

"You got too many melons in the car!" I said.

But Walter fixed the tire, we crawled in over the melons, and we finally got back to Milwaukee.

"Thank God!" papa said when we got home.

The watermelons stood the trip fine and Walter took most of them to Chicago. Our melon was so big, I had to cut it in two to get it in the refrigerator.

In May of 1947 sixteen-year-old Tom came to live with us. His mother had died a year or two earlier and his foster mother knew Mrs. Daniels, our upstairs neighbor. The woman wanted to take in girls so she asked Mrs. Daniels if she could take Tom, but she already had a girl so she came down and talked to me about it.

"Tom's a nice boy," Mrs. Daniels said. "He's quiet, respectful. I think you'd get along."

"I don't see how we can take a boy, with Ora," I said.

"I'll be glad to take Ora if you take the boy," she said.

"Ora?" The idea surprised me, but Ora was growing up and wouldn't be with us much longer, no matter what. Besides, she liked Mrs. Daniels. We asked Ora how she felt about the idea and she didn't object, seemed happy that this boy named "Tom" would have a place to live. I think foster kids have feeling for other kids without parents.

"You know we'll always be right downstairs if you want to talk," I said.

So Ora moved upstairs and Tom came. He was tall, gentle, serious. Right away, it seemed like there was a bond between us. I was redecorating Ora's old room for him, so Tom's bed was in the dining room for a few days. There was a fluffy pillow and thick comforter on the bed and the first night Tom got into bed he pulled the covers up and grinned, "Just like a cloud!"

Papa was very fond of Tom, but his memory kept traveling back to old times and a son and grandson named "Ben." He always forgot and called Tom "Ben." My brother Ben had died almost ten years earlier—I never saw him but once after he went to Kansas City, about 1918—but that name stayed with papa.

"Ben?!" I said when he used the wrong name.

"Oh, you know who I'm talkin' about!" he said.

After a few days Tom said, "Mrs. Heard, can I call you 'Mom'?"

"You sure can!" I said. Oh, my, it felt good to be called "Mom!"

Tom was ambitious. Days, he went to school and three nights a week he ran an elevator at a hotel. And on the other nights he did odd jobs at another hotel! I didn't think he was getting enough sleep, but he didn't complain. Then one day his teacher called.

"Mrs. Heard," she said, "Tom's a very nice boy, but I don't know what to do with him—he falls asleep in class."

But Tom didn't want to cut back on his work hours. We got along so well, and after a few months Tom begged us to let his brother, Dennis, come to live with us. Willard and I talked it over and soon we had two boys, but Dennis wasn't with us long before he moved to California.

When Tommy had friends over, those boys sat spellbound, listening to papa talk about the Bible, Arkansas and his escapades. And he told a joke a minute.

It was about that year that we heard my brother, Henry, had died in St. Louis. He'd visited us at the teashop once in the '30s and was my favorite brother, but I had to tell my sister-in-law I was sorry I couldn't come to the funeral because I couldn't leave papa alone. He was almost ninety-five and failing and I never left him alone anymore.

Christmas was special in 1949 because Tom bought us our first television—a Halicraft. Willard and I were excited about the snow we could see on the screen, but papa just nodded, like he couldn't say much anymore.

He had an old black leather pocketbook with a silver clasp that he'd brought from Washington. I bought his clothes and other necessities out of his monthly pension, but I gave him five dollars every month and he'd saved quite a bit that he carried in his purse. He was proud of that. About two days after Christmas, papa brought his pocketbook and handed it to me. He was particular about the purse and when he gave it to me I knew what it meant. Then he took to his bed.

Papa had pain and began hollering, so I called the doctor and he had Tom pick up a pain-killer at his office. I'd given papa one of the tablets and was sitting in a chair by his bed while he slept. He was sleeping, breathing gently, and then he just stopped. We buried him on New Year's Eve Day, 1949.

Willard and I meditated a lot. So many of our friends and relatives had died, made the transition, I don't know what we'd have done without a spiritual life to hold onto.

We were praying hard when Tom joined the Army and went off to the Korean War, about 1953. He was trained to be a radio operator, but it seems like soldiers never get to do what they go to school to learn to do and he wound up driving half-tracks on roads so narrow, trucks couldn't pass each other. He wrote about trenches the Koreans used for bathrooms, and dogs dressed out, hanging on lines like sides of beef. All the while, we prayed for him and at last Tom came home. After he'd been home a few days, he told me a story while we were sitting in the living room. I was darning socks.

"One day I was sitting on the back of a half-track while we were going down a dirt road," he said. "It was full of ruts, like all of them."

"Like North Avenue in spring," I said and slid the glass egg behind a hole.

"Worse, Mom!" he said. "A lot worse! Anyhow, all of a sudden something told me to duck. I didn't hear any voice, no

131

words, but I just knew I had to duck and I did. Just then a huge steel arm swung over where my head had been—it had broken loose from the truck."

"Tom!" I stared at him and he nodded.

"If I hadn't ducked when I did, I'd have been killed," he said. "I think it was your prayers that saved me, Mom. Something bigger than both of us made me put my head down!"

A NEW HOME

Willard was still at IBM and Tom went to work as a longshoreman at the Milwaukee Harbor, while I kept house and took in short-term foster children. We'd lived on Vine Street a long time, but I couldn't get used to renting. It was kind of a dream Willard and I had, to have a place of our own again. In 1958, I saw an ad for a duplex: **"$200 down—$75 a month payment."**

"I think we can handle that!" I said to Willard.

So the next day we went to talk to Mr. Zimmerman at Ettenheim and Zimmerman Real Estate Company, then we went to see the house on Seventeenth Street. It was roomy and well-kept; the man who'd owned it had done a lot to it before he died of a heart attack. Willard told the people at IBM about our plans to buy the house, and some of the managers wanted to check the papers to make sure no one was taking us in on the deal. Everything was okay, and in a few weeks we were in our own home for the first time in over twenty years. I don't know who was most excited—Willard, Tom or me!

Tom's grandmother, Rosie Jacobson, was getting old and being moved from one relative to another, and shortly after we moved, Tom begged me to let Rosie live in the spare room upstairs.

"You sure do like me to take people in!" I teased.

"Grandma's getting old—she needs to stay put," he said.

So Rosie came to live with us. It helped because she was a nice old lady and it gave us some rent income, too. Rosie was psychic, and I'll never forget the day I was on a ladder putting up curtains at the window on the back stairway while she stood and watched.

"Who's that pretty lady with the white hair that's always around you?" she said.

I thought she was talking about a friend, Mrs. Johnson, and I said, "Some of the neighbors, I reckon."

"She carries her arm like this," Rosie said, and held her arm across her stomach.

And I knew she knew who she was talking about—that was mama! Rosie never saw mama in her life, didn't know anything about her, because mama'd been dead long before I knew Rosie. Mama was out of proportion because of having one arm, and she'd carried it across her stomach for balance, just like Rosie showed me. There was no way for Rosie to know that, but I could often feel mama's presence, sixteen years after she'd died. And Rosie could see her!

Rosie was known for her healing hands, and the last time I went to vote at the Fourteenth Street School, I was flying down the street, hit a raised part of the sidewalk, and went down. The first thing I did was look around to see if anybody saw me. A man driving by stopped and called, "Lady, are you hurt?"

"No!" I said.

But my knee was blue, all swollen and painful. I limped home and went right up to Rosie.

"Rosie, would you look at my knee?" I hobbled to her rocker.

She bent over, peered at my knee, then shook her head.

"Mmm! Don't look like you'll be dancin' tonight!" she said. Then she ran her hand above my knee—about an inch above it, not on it—and said a prayer. My knee went down right there, and I never had trouble with it.

Rosie stayed with us for two or three years, then she got restless and moved into a highrise. We always said she had one foot in the road—she didn't like to stay in one place too long. Later, she went into a nursing home and was there for several years before she died.

We got word that Minnie died in the '50s. Willard retired from IBM in 1959, but otherwise life went on like always. During the '60s we kept up the house, had a few parties and tried to keep in touch with old friends who were left and with some of our foster children. Tom still lived with us; he never married, and he was truly a son to us. Joanne Holly had been married quite a few years before she had a baby; she was about thirty-five when Stephanie was born. And I gave Stephie papa's bedroom set.

As time passed, prayer and meditation meant more and more to me. So many needed my prayers, including Willard. He had emphysema and got so he had to sleep with his mouth open. Ever since he'd had pleurisy when he was a child, he had weakness in his lungs. He began getting medical treatment in the '60s, and maybe he should have had it earlier, but Dr. Carhart had died and we didn't have a doctor for a long time. It was hard to replace him.

Tom had a deep faith, too. He belonged to St. Benedict the Moor Catholic Church that served the poor (it serves free meals six nights a week, with people from churches all over the city and suburbs bringing food). I remember St. Ben's as a little mission down the street from Octavia's flat on Prairie Street. Tom always liked to hear stories about the old days, so I'd tell him about St. Ben's.

"I didn't know anything about Catholics when I came to Milwaukee," I told him. "Hadn't had any in Washington and hadn't hardly heard of the Catholic Church. So I came here and one day in walked this man to visit Octavia and Willard. He had a great long red beard, and I thought, 'Who is that?'. Then Octavia introduced him as Father Stephen from St. Benedict's Church.

"Father Stephen was a lovely man, visited people in the neighborhood, whether or not they were Catholic, and we got to be good friends. Willard and I went over to the mission quite often and sat on the long plank benches and prayed."

So it was natural to visit with Father Alexis from St. Ben's when he came to visit Tom. Pretty soon I was telling him about the bookrack of religious literature we'd had at the teashop: it had started with the "Daily Word" from Unity, then some Christian Science booklets, then two Catholic papers. I read them all! I began asking Father Alexis questions and Willard and I'd have long discussions with him.

Finally, one day I said, "Father, do you think you could give us instructions?" So Father Alexis came to the house to teach us, and in 1974 or '75 we became Catholic. But I still believed in reincarnation—I still do.

By that time I was tiring easily and knew I had the same heart trouble that had killed mama and my sisters. I was eighty-two when I was in the hospital with heart trouble. The doctor said I'd never be able to do housework again.

"Mrs. Heard," he said, "I think you should consider going into a nursing home."

MARIAN CATHOLIC HOME

Marian Catholic Home was about five years old and only about two miles from our house, but my heart just about burst at the thought of going into an institution.

"I won't go unless you go with me," I said to Willard.

"This place wouldn't seem like home without you, Reg," he said. "Tom can take care of it."

So Tom took us to the home and we had a tour. It was neat, clean and everyone seemed friendly, so we set a date to move in.

I'll never forget the day we came: February 2nd, 1976. Groundhog Day, and ten degrees below zero! In the morning, we waited for Tom to warm the car before we put on our coats, but our suitcases were already by the front door when Tom came back in the house.

"Car won't start!" he said. "I'll have to call a cab." We sat while Tom phoned one cab company after another. My mind was whirling.

I don't want to go—the house is so warm...

Tom kept calling and finally got a cab driver who said he'd be right over. Slowly, we put on our coats...

I know it was part of the plan, but—oh, honey!—if I could tell you how I felt when we walked in this place. I was bewildered, felt empty inside. An aide met us, led us to the elevator and took us up to second floor. We stepped out in front of the nurses' desk, and they took us halfway down a long hall to a room on the north wing: 221. In the room, the aide began to help us unpack.

"Thank you anyway, we can do it," I said, and after she showed us the bathroom, she left.

We were quiet as we unpacked, hung up clothes and put our personal things in strange drawers—a small nightstand for

Willard and one for me. A nurse came in and talked to us, then two aides came to take us to lunch. They must have been short of chairs on our wing. For our first meal, they took us to separate dining rooms at opposite ends of the long corridor. Willard was taken to the south end and I went to the north.

Everybody in the dining room was strange. I didn't eat much, my stomach was in such a commotion, and when I got back to our room, Willard was vomiting in the bathroom; he'd gotten sick in the other dining room. I think it was nerves, being away from me in a strange place. From then on, we always ate together. It was hard to pray that night. All I could do was rest in God.

In the days to come we didn't talk much. Willard and I never did talk a lot, but we communicated—we understood how the other was feeling. Beginning life in the nursing home was the strangest thing we'd ever done, even stranger than going to the rooming house after we lost the teashop, because Bessie and most of our friends and relatives were dead and we didn't have anyone to lean on but Tom. Hollys, Reverend Fisher, mama, papa—they were all gone.

Leaning on nurses, aides and social workers was a new way of life. The staff was nice to us from the start and didn't push us too far. We could do pretty much what we wanted to, but it was like we'd been gearing up for something all our life and now the brake was jammed. At least, that's how it seemed at first. But I tried not to think negative thoughts: I believe you become what you claim. If you claim negation, you become negative. I didn't know why we had to be there, but I was sure it was part of the Plan.

So in the next weeks, I'd smile and say "Hello" to everyone, and people got to know us. There weren't many wheelchairs around because most of the patients could walk then, and some of them started dropping in our room to visit. Tom came every day and took us out a lot, and over the months a wonderful thing happened: the Home began to feel like home. There was a lot going on. When Elizabeth Mitchell became the Home's first 100-year-old, they had a big birthday party and Governor Martin Schreiber came.

Willard and I were always having company, even had parties with china and linens from home. Willard attracted people like a magnet—no one was a stranger to him! That New Year's

Eve, and all the ones to come, we had a big champagne party in our room.

One year, for one of my birthdays the Home had a big party for me and invited the Milwaukee Courier, the minority newspaper, to write a story. Everyone was looking for a black reporter to show up, and it was a joke on us because when they came, the reporter and photographer were both white! They did a good job, though, gave me quite a spread.

We had six-and-a-half beautiful years at Marian Home, but by 1982 something was just pushing me to get out. Willard didn't want to leave.

"We've got it nice, Reg," he said. "Got our meals, everyone's good to us—" He didn't say it, but he was getting more frail and it was harder for him to breathe.

"I think it's time for us to go home." Nothing could make me swerve.

The Home gave a big party for us before we left, and the department heads signed a card saying, "You can always come back here to live." It was July 27, 1982.

At first, it was wonderful to be home. But I soon knew things would never be the same. I guess it's true: "You can never go home again." Our hearts and spirits were young, but Willard and I were both old and sick in our bodies, and it was an effort to cook and do housework. We had twin beds and at night when he was down, Willard had awful coughing attacks.

During the days we both were in bed a lot. I don't know what it was, but during that time I began hearing music, and it was always the same song: "The Battle Hymn of the Republic."

"Do you hear music playing?" I asked Willard and Tom.

"No," Willard said.

"I don't hear anything," Tom said.

It would go away for awhile and then a day or two later I'd hear it again, but it got so I quit mentioning it. I was going down mentally and physically, and I prayed to God to send someone to me—I needed a woman to talk to, to be a friend. All those years, I'd still called for mama's spirit when I needed her and she'd come to me. One night, Willard had gone to sleep and I finally drifted off—I never needed much

137

sleep. Then I had this dream that took place in the flat where mama had died, on Vine Street. The dream seemed more like a vision...

> they came into the living room...
> papa was walking a little behind mama
> and had a hat set rakish on his head
> mama wore a wide hat and a cape
> like we made to cover her arm
> 'We're here,' she said
> I reached up and took the hat
> 'You look like a girl in this hat'
> I said, looking at her close
> she was so tired...

After that, I quit calling for mama. They say it's not good to grieve after your departed because you keep them from resting or going on. So I said, "I won't do that any more." And I haven't called her since.

Then Willard developed cancer in a lung and he was in pain so much of the time, I prayed to God to take his suffering away; I wanted him to die before I did. I didn't want to go through all of that by myself, but I knew he wasn't able to cope by himself. I'd always managed our business and he wouldn't have known where to start with insurance and papers.

Willard had one spell after another in the winter of '83-'84, and was in and out of Deaconess Hospital. When he was home I was taking care of him, feeding him and lifting him and my heart was giving out. I was sick in bed one day, and Willard might have thought I was dying because he started crying and came and fell across the bed on me.

"I won't let them take you away from me! I won't let them take you!" he said, with such strong willpower.

"Honey, I'm not going to leave you," I said, and held him so tight it seemed like his breathing was mine.

But I got to the place where I couldn't lift him, and he had to be hospitalized again. I think there's no need in keeping people alive unless you can give them some measure of health. If a person has a terminal disease, my doctor doesn't believe in keeping you living just for the sake of living. He was on vacation and he'd just got home the Sunday night when they took Willard to the hospital.

A surgeon had phoned and wanted to operate on Willard right away, and he asked my position, and of course I didn't have any sense.

"I want you to do anything that can help him," I said.

Then my doctor got back and called and said, "If I were you, I wouldn't let him operate, because it won't do anything but prolong Willard's suffering."

So I changed it. And anybody who knew Willard thought I'd done the right thing. Everyone loved Willard. He was so good to people, he'd never say anything bad about anyone. But Willard never came home again.

Putting Willard back in the nursing home was the hardest thing I ever did in my life—he wanted to die in his own bed. But I knew the doctor was right: I couldn't lift Willard any more. So we put him back in Marian Catholic Home, and Tom and I went to be with him every day. Willard died shortly after he went there, on March 9, 1984. (Regie's voice was hushed and she wiped tears from her eyes as she told about Willard's transition.)

I've never told this to anybody, but I had the strangest feeling in the funeral home when I walked up to my husband's casket and saw him lying there. Something said, "Call him! Call him!" I used to say, "Willard!" and he'd always wake up. And I had to use all my willpower to keep from calling him. I didn't want him back in all that pain that he had. The body dies, the soul doesn't—I believe that—but I had to fight with all my strength to keep from calling him.

A NEW DREAM

When we went back home after the funeral, I felt like I was half gone, I was so lonely. We had a girl in to help with the cooking, but I was afraid to be alone whenever Tom left for even a short time, and my strength was gone. Except for Tom, I was alone on an island.

All I could do was pray to God, "Please send a woman who can be a friend." For months I prayed for a woman friend t' appear. It must have been in late fall when I had a dream:

an Oriental Indian with a shaved head
stood in our middle room
—the center room—
between the kitchen and living room
he wore a maroon sweater and street clothes
and looked wise
beyond earth's ages

I woke up and it was wonderful, I felt so good; it's impossible to describe how peaceful I felt. Whoever this was, he would take care of everything. And from the dream, I knew that I was to become centered and develop inner strength, so I made a decision: I moved back to Marian Catholic Home on Dec. 14, 1984—nine months after Willard died.

Everyone here has always been good to me, and when nurses from other floors found out I was back, they stopped in to see me. Tom came almost everyday (and still does), but I still prayed to God for a woman friend to appear. When you (the writer) came into my life three weeks after I moved back, the minute you walked in the room I knew you were the answer. I think God wanted me to meet you: you're part of the Plan. You started me living again.

The first thing you said that day was, "Mrs. Heard, I'm a volunteer and a professional writer. I'm researching aging minorities in Milwaukee and Dr. Bonjean said she thought I should meet you. Would you like me to write your life story, for a little journal for you?"

And I said, "Why don't you sit down? I think I'd like that..."

14
Regie's Philosophy:
Aim At the Stars

EDITOR'S NOTE: Regie Robinson was salutatorian of her class at Haygood Seminary, and helped valedictorian Essie Burge with homework. With typical humor, Regie chose as the theme of her paper, "Aim at the stars, although you may hit a treetop." During her long life, she learned to move out from under the trees before she took aim. Her mental and spiritual goals are higher than ever, and some of her dreams and thoughts follow.

* * *

I was getting ready to die before (the writer) came along. I had no interest in anything, and when we began talking about the past, it was like I was renewed again. So many memories I'd forgotten came back as I talked. They were always in my mind, but they never came to mind.

* * *

Young people should ask their parents and grandparents all the questions they can. Suppose I hadn't asked mama so many questions. And what if she hadn't talked to me? It's important for families to write things down.

* * *

The only consolation you have after a loved one dies is the memory of your relationship.

I'm nearly ninety-three and I don't feel old—sick, sometimes, but not old. That's one thing that shows we're spiritual beings: I'm the same person I was when I was a child. I know more and have more experience, but I don't feel different inside. I'm the same I.

* * *

After I brought mama and papa here, they were lonely. I'd advise anyone with aging parents to keep them in familiar surroundings as long as possible.

* * *

It's awful to be alone, if you were attached to your husband. Some women can change husbands like they change dresses.

* * *

I always prided myself that I could change, but since Willard's death any kind of change bothers. But we've got to accept change: it's coming all the time. Look at nature—trees and grass change.

* * *

Fear held me back many times in life. I've made up my mind I'm not going to be afraid of new people or situations. Older people should get out and have new experiences.

* * *

We limit ourselves by letting fear hold us back. Years ago when I was in deep meditation, I felt myself getting bigger and going into a huge circle, but I pulled back because I was afraid. I know now, I missed an opportunity.

* * *

You can sense a spirit of love—that's why you like certain people. We're all spiritual beings and a part of God, but some are more developed than others.

142

Spiritual understanding is the most important thing in my life; it's different from intellectual understanding. Love and spiritual understanding bring a wisdom that erases all prejudice—against a race, religion or age.

* * *

Dreams have always been important to me. After I was an adult, several times I dreamt I was in a long white gown, on the portico of a huge building with white marble columns. I never saw anyone else or my face, because I was in my body, walking and sometimes leaning against a pillar; I felt so comfortable there.

* * *

I didn't dream of Willard after he died, and thought it was strange because we were very close. Then a year after his death, in March of 1985, I had a dream:

> I was sitting in Willard's chair in a house
> and he knelt on the floor beside me...
> he looked young as I caressed his hair
> -it was black in a short crewcut-
> "You never wore your hair like this before," I said
> he didn't answer, but got up and walked out the door
> I went to the window and saw him walking
> up a dirt road   he fell and struggled to get up
> he reached out his arms toward where the road led
> but he kept falling...

From that dream, I got the impression that he was trying to go on and I was interfering with his progress. It meant I was to stop grieving and let him go, so I quit thinking about his death all the time and holding him back. And I quit holding myself back with grief.

* * *

All religions are looking for the same thing. They're like spokes of a wagonwheel, coming closer together toward the hub, and in the center, they all go together in one.

143

Anything the Indians worshipped, like the sun, was just as much God to them as our God is to us, because they were worshipping something higher than they were.

* * *

If God is everywhere, then we're not separated from God, we're just sticking out in visibility. Your real self is invisible. When the body wears out, the soul gives it up and keeps developing, getting reborn until it becomes a perfect expression of love. That's what reincarnation is about.

* * *

Love is the most important thing in the world. Not the rolling in bed kind—love that is everything good.

* * *

When I'm awake in the middle of the night, I meditate and sometimes get unfoldment. I was always an "I'm from Missouri" sort of person and everything had to be proved to me. Now I have a realization of my divine nature. Mostly, it comes in the night.

* * *

It doesn't disturb me when someone cries out at night—I feel sorry for anyone who seems lost. I try to open myself to be a channel by meditating on whoever is yelling out, and mentally telling the individual that God is present. A woman up the hall sounded like a lost child, and I'd imagine I was holding her in my arms, crooning to her like a mother does to a baby. Often, after I'd pictured her going to sleep for awhile, she was quiet. In the years I've been here, I've done that with a lot of people.

* * *

Afterword

by Bonnie Langenhahn

Regie Heard epitomizes the inner healing that writing therapy can generate when writer and storyteller merge minds. "No matter how badly I felt when we began, I was so interested when we were working that I never felt sick then," she told me two years after we began her life story.

When I first entered her room that January in 1984, she looked up and we both experienced recognition. By the end of the first interview, I sensed that this journal would be more far-reaching than any of dozens I'd done. By the second interview, we were discussing dreams and mystical experiences, and I asked Regie if she would like to work on a book of her life. She immediately agreed.

Hers is not the usual journal, but it is a model of what is possible, regardless of age. In the following months we met weekly, talking for two or three hours while the tape recorder ran. As laughter punctuated memories of 'possums and pouncing on frost-filled melons, a sparkle came to Regie's eyes. Too, at times there were tears and memories that made me push the "pause" button on the recorder.

At home, the challenge was in organizing the material from a mounting pile of tapes. Without a computer, editing would have been an insurmountable task. Unlike most journals, much was culled and the book represents about half of the conversations on tape. My distance from the home also meant that I got many pertinent facts by phone.

The narrative voice is less "hers" than "ours." Regie didn't like such dialect as "I reckon" in print—which she was unaware that she said, and I found charming. So we merged minds and changed the voice somewhat. Such brain-storming showed the potential of creativity into advanced age: Regie was involved with each decision and proofreading. On about the fifth draft, I suggested that I simulate dialogue and Regie's reaction was positive: "Good idea! It would read more like a story, wouldn't it?" I said I hoped it would. To my amazement, at times the book's characters threatened to run away with me. To Regie's delight, they brought life to her life. "Bonnie, that's exactly the way they talked! It's the way they **were**!"

To us, the most important result of our work has been the growth in our relationship. Regie's faith in me taught me to trust my intuition, and led us to love, mutuality and a sense of playfulness with life that continues. Recently I noted that we never had an argument during the entire project. "We could never have a fight!" she declared.

Our growing attunement of mind and spirit meant that our act of creation became charged with a sense of the sacred, in the midst of writing of seances, numbers men and bootlegging! Serendipitous events made it sacred play, and the scribed journal of an elderly woman spiraled into a divine task.

For those who wonder what led me into this field, I offer a brief history. After years as an x-ray techician, homemaker and freelance writer, my pursuit of writing as therapy began in January, 1982, when I began a book discussion group as a volunteer at a local nursing home. I discovered joy in working with the elderly that led me to a gerontology course at Cardinal Stritch College, in addition to studies at Mount Mary College toward a degree in professional writing. For my paper, I researched the potential of writing with the elderly or disabled, including positive results of multisensory motivation of group poems I was doing at the nursing home.

In January, 1983, I was granted a journal-writing internship at Marian Catholic Home, sponsored by the Mount Mary English Department. While writing the journals, I had a sense of letting go of self-ego as I discovered that recognizing the higher being in each participant was basic to capturing his/her total dimension on paper. As lives unfolded, the "writing" residents' self-esteem soared and I knew that what I was doing made a difference, especially when one man died and his widow asked me to finish his life story with the family.

By 1984 (the year of Willard's death), I was invited to present a research paper at the annual conference of the Wisconsin Academy of Sciences, Arts and Letters in Madison. The paper was about the need for a new profession: Writing Therapy.

I graduated from Mount Mary in May and, to complete the gerontology minor, began planning an independent study of aging minorities under the guidance of Joanne Poehlmann, Ph.D., chairperson of the Behavioral Science Department. Accompanied by Wilma Robinson, a friend who is an African-American, I received permission from the Milwaukee

County Department of Social Services to gather life histories from voluntary participants in government apartments for the elderly.

So while Regie was praying for a friend, I was taping life histories of elderly black women. At age 48, I was the first student to complete the gerontology minor, and the Mount Mary Behavioral Science department gave me a small award on December 10, 1984. It was the same week that Regie re-entered Marian Catholic Home.

With some doubts about my future and the practicality of what I was doing, I continued to be drawn toward using writing as therapy and the first week in January, 1985, I went into Dr. Bonjean's office and told her I had decided to continue motivating and writing life histories.

"We have a resident who could add a lot to your minority study," she said, "and I think she will be interested in what you're doing. She's a remarkable woman..."

And "remark-able" Regie was! As work progressed, she became more than a link with the past. To me, she was a bridge—between races, generations, North and South, Eastern and Western religions, the secular and sacred, the conscious and superconscious mind, inertia and creativity and, ultimately, between life and death.

It is our hope that her story and our "merging-minds" way of writing will motivate families, writers and professionals who work with the aging to listen to and record the lives of their elders, because their lives are part of our future.

TRAVELS, INTO CREATIVITY — and WASHINGTON

Regie's creativity is not stopping. When stiff fingers allow, she now writes thoughts and dreams in a private notebook.

For socialization, about twice a month we do a private "Regie review" of a restaurant. And we seem to always have a foot in the road. We never get lost, but there are always surprises. Recently, we toured Madison with my mother and ended up in front of the governor's mansion at the invitation of Sharon Erb.

The next day we headed west along the Wisconsin River and into the hills east of Gays Mills, where blossoms hung like cotton tufts on 1,000 acres of apple trees in the Kickapoo Valley. We roamed west to The Great River Road along the

147

Mississippi flowing spring-syrup strong between pine-pocked bluffs the color of Indian pudding, and coasted through Prairie du Chien and over a new concrete-sure bridge. It took the old thrill out of reaching MacGregor, Iowa, where houses cling to cliffs, but Regie was thrilled with her first visit to that state. "I always thought Iowa was all corn fields!"

Back in Grant County, Wisconsin, we chugged up and down roller-coaster streets in the old lead mining town of Mineral Point before stopping at a bakery for cornish pasties like miners had carried for lunch.

A week later she went to a nonagenarian lunch in Greenfield at columnist Helen Mollinger's, where friends in their nineties mentally sparred with those in their eighties and toasted each other with champagne. "I didn't meet anyone who looked ninety!" she said. Neither did I.

Next, Regie had an appointment with a masseuse in wooded Elm Grove, west of Milwaukee. Marion Marsh, R.N., certified massage therapist and health counselor, worked on her for an hour as Asian Indian woodwinds played in the background— Regie's choice of tape. Marion exclaimed over her remarkable condition and ability to relax. Afterward, Regie ambled into the living room and settled into a rocker with a cup of tea, saying, "I feel brand new." She added that she wished every old person could have a massage.

A year earlier, in 1986, we both could have used a massage at the end of a day of driving. In January, I'd asked Regie if she thought she could endure a trip to Arkansas, and it was all I could do to make her wait until spring. Wanting to do research for the book, we thought we chose the spring of '86. Looking back, maybe the year chose us.

In 1836, 150 years earlier, the U.S. Senate had adopted a bill that would admit Arkansas as the twenty-fifth state in the Union. Sixty-five years earlier, to the week, Regie had left Washington to catch a train north to marry Willard. Exactly forty years before, Regie and Willard had the "sand-in-the-radiator" trip with Walter, Aletha and papa.

So early on April 21, looking as if we were heading for two months in Europe instead of eight days in the South, we pushed a wheelchair reeling under Regie's two large suitcases, straw hat and overnight bag down to my Reliant. I helped

Regie into the front seat and an attendant figured out a formula for fitting the wheelchair, a small suitcase and the hat in the trunk. The rest went in the back seat with my luggage, cooler, camera bag and two sacks of munchies. On top of one of them I balanced two plastic bags of oversized muffins that Dolores Ludwig, former head nurse on second floor, had come in an hour early to give us.

Everyone waved and the sun shone as we headed for Illinois and Lincoln's New Salem State Park, a symbolic first lunch stop. As we drove on, Regie marveled at broad reaches of rolling fields and exclaimed, "You can go as fast as you want to here—that sign said, 'NO SPEED ZONE!'"

We were taking the long way to Washington, via Unity Village in northwestern Missouri because its literature had "turned my life around," Regie said. We paused in Hannibal, Missouri, near Mark Twain's birthplace and white picket fence facing the Mississippi River, then headed west.

Not having made any overnight trips since 1946, and **never** having stayed in a motel, Regie had been concerned about finding lodging, but by nightfall we were snug in a motel in Mexico, Missouri. If she was nervous because we were traveling alone, she didn't show it except to check that the door was locked every time I went to the car to unload a bag. The next day was a straight shot west to Unity Village, where we meditated in the 24-hour prayer room, had lunch, then left for Arkansas. Missouri's western border of dips and rills leveled out at Harry Truman's birthplace, then burgeoned into full valleys and hills toward the southern state line.

Near Diamond, we turned off the main road and drove miles back to George Washington Carver's birthplace deep in a valley between wooded hills. In that spot so peaceful that rustles of wind and songs of birds soared amplifier-strong, we felt one with the former slave who sought to live "in the spirit of a little child seeking only to know the truth and follow it." Reluctantly, we pushed on toward Arkansas.

At the edge of the Ozarks, our stomachs stormed for smoked razorback ribs before beginning the winding ascent to Eureka Springs, "little Switzerland of America." Pastel hued victorian homes hugging the hills and homelike smorgasbords gave Regie such a sense of security that by the second night she didn't check the motel door.

We'd decided to take a side trip to Hot Springs because of

149

her many summers there visiting Faye and Lilly. After a sixty-five year absence, Regie would have been totally disoriented if we hadn't found Bathhouse Row. We did, and the search for the Majestic Hotel and Pine Street was on. As I fought congested traffic untrained in southern hospitality we saw several hotels, one of which Regie thought resembled the old Majestic. Concentrating on driving, all I could see was a network of scaffolding scouring the front of the building. We drove until we were in a residential area, then turned back. Just before we reached the scaffold-hotel I saw a street sign.

"There's Pine Street!" I yelled and turned onto a blessedly quiet residential street of neat, mostly modern homes. "Does this look familiar?"

"Everything looks different," she said quietly, "but I think Faye and Lilly lived up this away." She was sitting on the edge of her seat, peering and pointing toward the left side of the street. Slowly we drove up the hill, then suddenly Regie said, "There on the left, I could swear that's the spot!"

I braked and looked across the street to where Regie was pointing. The ruins of an old house rose above concrete steps framed with weeds. "Do you think that's where Faye lived?"

"Lord, it's hard to tell, but that's where Ada's houses were," she said.

"I'll take a picture, in case," I said. It was a picturesque scene, with sun streaming through vines entwining boards that were rotting and returning to earth, enriching it for saplings sprouting up among weeds and wild flowers.

"I'm sure that's the spot," Regie said, "so that could be one of Ada's houses."

I nodded. No harm in enjoying the theory. After all, we weren't broadcasting it. Who'd believe a middle-aged stranger and an old woman who hadn't set foot in Hot Springs in nearly seventy years? Yipes! They must have hot springs in their heads! We continued up the street, passed a barefoot boy packing a string of fish, and found the highway that would lead to Regie's roots, to Washington.

"ENTERING WASHINGTON/ AN HISTORIC TOWN SETTLED BEFORE 1824/ RECONSTRUCTED BY ARKANSAS STATE PARKS and PIONEER WASHINGTON RESTORATION FOUNDATION" said a white sign under a tree. I didn't have a sense of driving into a town. Huge trees and shrubs dwarfed houses that were, as Regie had said, "all spread out."

150

We drove a few blocks and should have passed the site of her old home. Regie was on the edge of her seat, whispering, "Oh, my gosh! I don't see a thing I recognize! Where did all these hills come from?"

The road embankments were steep. "The yards used to be flat out to the road..." The white sand was gone. Later, we were told that new road construction cut into the hills and reddish clay replaced the sand. The Robinsons' home had burned down over thirty years earlier, as had the Royston house, so we decided to look for universal landmarks.

"Let's see if we can find the courthouse," Regie said. "It should be straight ahead and over a block or two." It was, standing red-brick solid, just as Regie remembered it. "If this hadn't been here, I'd have thought I'd gone crazy!"

We pulled up by the redwood stile and fence that used to be white as Regie exclaimed, "I've got to get out!" I helped her out and leaning on her cane, she walked to the stile. "Oh, my gosh!" she whispered and gazed, suspended in time. Then she pointed to a spot on the lawn and said, "They used to hang 'em over there." A sign explained a restoration project and showed sites of Greek-revival homes built to duplicate pre-Civil War originals. The courthouse now held the Southwest Arkansas Regional Archives, but it was closed for the day.

Regie in front of the former Washington Courthouse (1986)

We tracked down the Royston House, but Regie was confused and disappointed that it wasn't the elegant two-story home she had known, and it wasn't up the street from her old house. "Lord, Bonnie, if you didn't know me better, you'd think I was a liar!" She shook her head.

Next, following Regie's directions, we found the world's biggest magnolia tree. It wasn't in bloom, but burgeoned with green buds bigger than my thumb. A block away stood the old Confederate capitol, freshly painted white. Relieved to find her memories reinforced, Regie walked in front of the tree, then we drove past a blacksmith shop, reminder that the Bowie knife was designed here by James Black in 1831.

On the main road, I rolled down the window and asked two ebony-skinned boys where we might find any old people. They looked startled, but one said, "The next house on the left," and pointed. Thanking them, we pulled into a gravel drive and parked under a tree full of yellow flowers. I went up, knocked on the door and a slim, white-haired lady invited me in. Her name was Mary _____ and I told her about our journey, that we were going back to a motel near the highway and would be back the next day. Immediately, the kind stranger said that in the morning she would show us to Mary Margaret Haynes' home across the street from the former Robinson homestead.

Regie and I drove back to a Red Carpet Inn near the highway and checked in. It wasn't until we read the motel's postcard that we realized we were in Hope! "Oh, who'd ever have thought I'd be stayin' in a fine motel in Hope?" Regie laughed. At breakfast the next morning, she whispered, "This is the first time I ever ate in an integrated restaurant in Hope!" Maybe that was why the food tasted doubly good. She used the integrated restroom for good measure, then we drove into town for gas. Regie was nervous, slunk down on her seat and shaded her face, but a friendly station attendant told me how to get to the "old" depot and she sat up straighter. We drove around the train station, but the old depot was new to her, and the "Colored" entrance was gone. Later, we found out that this "old" depot was built after Regie moved North. We took the road back to Washington.

At the courthouse we found Mary Medearis, Director of the Southwest Arkansas Regional Archives, who arranged to have the gate opened so we could drive up to the back stairs of the building so Regie could easily walk in. While we searched for family records, she explained that the new Black History Museum was opening in one week, on the following Saturday. "I think the director, Mildred Smith, would like to talk to you," she said and made a phone call.

Within minutes, Mildred Smith walked in, and we couldn't have been placed in better hands. Thus began our re-discovery of some of the Washington Regie once knew.

Congenial Mary Margaret Haynes was a neighbor of Amelia and Nobie Robinson until they moved to Milwaukee. "They were wonderful people," she said. "Mr. Robinson was one of the most intelligent men I ever knew—he was always reading, except when he was working in his garden."

Next we picked up Mary, the lady who had helped us the evening before, and she, Miss Haynes and Mrs. Smith helped us find the remains of the old Robinson well.

Mary Margaret Haynes (left) and Mildred Smith (right) steadied Regie as she peered into the old family well made by Joe Green. (The man in the background lives in a house where the Robinson home stood.)

Our excursions took us to Marguerite Smith Moses, 84, whom Regie knew as a child, then to a banquet-size chicken lunch at Mildred Smith's modern farmhouse up the road from the spot where Haygood Seminary had stood.

We forgot about switching to daylight savings time, so on Sunday we were nearly an hour late when we strolled into Regie's former church, St. Paul's C.M.E., but everyone turned and murmured, "Welcome, sisters," to the tardy two and we were surrounded by music and love. The first man to extend his hand introduced himself as Julius Green.

"Was your father Joe Green, the brick-maker?" I asked.

Astonished, he grinned, "No, he was my granddaddy."

We taped up our trip by videotaping Mildred Smith interviewing Regie at her home and left on Monday morning.

And so the Arkansas we found in 1986 was a different state than Regie had last visited in 1946, and dramatically changed from her youth.

"I had many friends of both races," she said. "I wanted to record early days as I experienced them, and no maliciousness was intended. I'm so happy things have changed—imagine staying at a Red Carpet Inn!" It was symbolic of the red carpet welcome we received throughout Arkansas. On the way home that included a visit in West Memphis with her sister Minnie's son, daughter and their spouses, W. A. and Louise Morrow and Cecile and William Earlye.

To add new states to Regie's travels, we returned through western Tennessee and Kentucky, and arrived home at 11:00 p.m. on April 29. Later, I realized it was exactly fifty years after Regie walked out of the teashop for the last time, and sixty-five years from the night when she missed the train to her wedding.

A year later, in April, 1987, a story about Regie, our book and trip appeared in The Milwaukee Journal and she received calls and letters from readers: Bernard Givens' father was the maintenance man at the Urban League building when Regie did the meal planning for the first government-sponsored nursery school in the 1930's; Mrs. Walters had been a 19-year-old bride, living up the street from the Lutz mansion four years before it became a teashop; and Nathan Weinberg, a resident of the Milwaukee Jewish Home, wrote that Regie's story brought back memories of the Butterfly Theater and Surf Restaurant.

The most serendipitous call came from Arthur Lewis of Milwaukee. He had never heard of Regie Heard, but when he read her story he wondered if she knew his mother because she was a Washington native. Introducing himself, he told Regie his mother's maiden name.

"You must be Bessie Maddox' boy!" Regie said. "I remember when you were a baby!" Astonishingly, Lilly Dangerfield (Faye's mother) and Aunt Ada were his mother's sisters!

My follow-up phone call to Mr. Lewis revealed his amazement at Regie's memory and details she knew of his family. And she told of our visit to Hot Springs. Did he know anything about the deserted house on Pine Street?

"I own it," he said. "It was Aunt Ada's, and I was born there in 1914. We lived with her in the two-story house, and her little house was next door. When she died, Ada left it to my mother, and she left it to me, but the foundation wasn't good any more and it wasn't worth saving."

Now Mr. Lewis plans to visit Arkansas. And he's going to tape Regie for some of his family history.

Ruins of the Hot Springs house

So much for hot springs in an old lady's head!

Willard and Regie at Marian Catholic Home, 1981

155

Above (left to right):
Papa Nobie Robinson, 94,
Tom Williams, 17,
and Willard Heard, 55

Above right: Regie, 54

Right: Mama Amelia Robinson, 75

156

Regie, 92   Milwaukee Journal Photo

About the Authors...

REGIE HEARD and her husband Willard were entrepreneurs in 1926-1936, a period of time that was not noted for encouraging free enterprise among minority people. The Angel Food Teashop, the Heard's elegant and unique restaurant, was located in a Milwaukee mansion and enjoyed a prestigious reputation among national celebrities and regional dignitaries.

The 93-year-old resident of Marian Catholic Home celebrated the completion of *REGIE'S LOVE* by beginning a new journal.

BONNIE LANGENHAHN, Menomonee Falls, Wisconsin, holds a Cum Laude B.A. in English Communication Arts and a gerontology minor from Mount Mary College, Milwaukee. She is editor of *THE WRITE AGE,* first magazine of writing therapy, and gives workshops, motivating writing with music, relaxation and multisensory methods.